MIDWIVES OF AN UNNAMED FUTURE

MIDWIVES OF AN UNNAMED FUTURE

Spirituality for Women in Times of Unprecedented Change

Mary Ruth Broz, RSM

Barbara Flynn

Photographs by Jean Clough

acta
PUBLICATIONS

MIDWIVES OF AN UNNAMED FUTURE

Spirituality for Women in Times of Unprecedented Change

Mary Ruth Broz, RSM, and Barbara Flynn
with photography by Jean Clough

Edited by Gregory F. Augustine Pierce and Nicole Kramer
Cover design by Tom A. Wright
Text design and typesetting by Patricia A. Lynch

Published by
ACTA Publications
5559 W. Howard Street
Skokie, IL 60077
(800) 397-2282
www.actapublications.com

Library of Congress Number: 2005936966
Printed in Canada
ISBN 10: 0-87946-293-0
ISBN 13: 978-0-87946-293-2
Year 10 09 08 07 06
Printing 10 9 8 7 6 5 4 3 2 1

CONTENTS

PHOTOGRAPHS BY JEAN CLOUGH

DEDICATION

Dedicated to the Women of Wellstreams
who have midwived us

And to granddaughters
Ellie, Caroline and Clare

And grandnieces
Katie and Elizabeth

With hope that your future
will see in you
The Feminine Face of God
and welcome you as partners
in a process of change

L ittle did the two of us know when we first met each other more than twenty years ago that we were in labor. All we did know was that the changes we both longed for and the questions we both carried could no longer be ignored:

"How can we relate to a God who seems so removed from our ordinary lives?"

"How can we stay faithful to ourselves in a church that consistently discounts women's experiences?"

"Where do we go to get replenished, to heal in times of confusion and grief?"

"What are we being asked to do in order to have a spirituality worth passing on to future generations?"

"Are there new ways of being church — places where women can tell their stories, where we can offer reverence to the Earth and celebrate her seasons and cycles, hold on to our belief that all is sacred, and breathe new life into age-old spiritual truths?"

We are both spiritual directors, though coming from different lifestyles: Barbara as a married woman and Mary Ruth as a Sister of Mercy. We knew that we were voicing the pain and concerns of the many different women who shared our journey.

Although we recognized we could not do *everything* in order to bring about the changes we hoped for, we did know that we could do *something*. There was no turning back. We began to dream a dream and eventually opened Wellstreams, a center for feminine spirituality. Over a twelve-year period, more than 400 circles of women came together to find their voice, their courage, and fresh energy for their work. Together with these women, we struggled to discover how we were being called to bring something new to birth.

The women who joined these circles were women like ourselves in that they refused to settle for the way things were: young women and older women; women juggling a professional life outside the home as well as stay-at-home moms; women who were hanging on to formal religion by a thread; and women from many different spiritual traditions who cared deeply for their faith communities but were struggling to survive. Some had been speaking their truth for many years, while others were finding their voice for the very first time.

What they all had in common was that they knew they needed something more. They wanted to deepen their own spirituality and were eager to find kindred spirits, knowing that they needed one another to move through the work of change. These were thoughtful, dedicated women who found a way to carve out time in the midst of soccer schedules and board meetings to come to the well and take a sip that would sustain them for the work ahead.

But this book is not only about them. It is about us, all of us. It is our belief that as women we need one another more than ever to bring forth a future still unclear and unable to be named. We all need resources. We need hope. And we need to know the circle is getting larger. Whether you choose to read this book alone or gather to read it with a few others, we hope you will soon discover that *Midwives of an Unnamed Future* offers you a way of experiencing feminine spirituality from the inside out. It is meant to both empower and nurture *you*.

We designed each chapter as a ritual, simply for the purpose of reminding you that the themes go deeper than words. Each chapter begins with the invitation to carve out your own sacred space and imagine yourself as part of a larger circle of women who are on the journey with you. Music, poetry, words and symbol are woven together around a common theme to help you tap into that place where you can hear the Spirit whisper: "I am about to do a new thing; now it springs forth, do you not perceive it?" (Isaiah 43:19).

From our own experience, the two of us have come to know that a process this simple has the power of taking us places we never expected to go. We did not intend to write a book, any more than we intended to open a center for feminine spirituality, but we soon learned that "calls" have a life of their own. Left to ourselves, we could easily have become paralyzed by our own demons:

"Are we saying anything new?"

"Maybe we should just forget it."

"Maybe our experience is unique to us."

"Should we just call the project off?"

But we knew there was more at work than ourselves. The Spirit continued to nudge us on: "Don't forget that each small piece is necessary for the larger conversation." Therefore, we offer our little piece of wisdom to the larger pool of resources on feminine spirituality as a way of supporting women like yourself, whom we believe are called upon to be midwives of an unnamed future.

As women, we know that some of the most important lessons are learned on the home front. Whether you call together a few friends or make this journey on your own, we invite you to pull up a chair, spread out a cloth, light a candle, and begin.

Mary Ruth Broz, RSM
Barbara Flynn
Chicago, Illinois

Each chapter of this book offers a mini-retreat of sorts, inviting you into sacred space and guiding you through a time of reflection. You can experience this book in many ways: alone in personal prayer, in the familiar setting of a small group of friends, or in a larger gathering such as a retreat group. In each chapter, there is a basic outline of the themes. You can follow the suggestions or alter them to fit your own needs as an individual or group.

You will find suggestions in each section for creating sacred space. Keep it simple! The invitation into sacred space is to remind you that the theme goes deeper than words. Give yourself permission to make it uniquely yours, adding your own personal touch to help you further enter into the experience.

Music is also a fitting companion to your journey into the mystery. Each section offers a suggested song to use. However, if the music to a song is not available, you may simply read the words aloud or choose another piece of music that helps guide you deeper into the theme.

Each chapter has a reflection on the theme being addressed. Read them at your own pace and return to them as often as you wish in the days and weeks ahead. The questions that follow can be used for personal journaling and quiet reflection or to launch a group discussion.

The closing reading and songs are offered as ways of bringing your time to conclusion and moving back into daily life. However, something else may feel more appropriate to you. Let your creativity well up as you enter this reflection process, making it unique to you or your group.

At the end of each section are suggestions for alternate ways of using the theme in group settings, including tips for applying the reflection to small or larger group gatherings. Still, we suggest that each participant have a book and an individual journal of her own so that personal prayer and reflection can take place before and after each session. There are also ideas included for a more in-depth shared ritual more appropriate for use by a circle of women. The reflections on the theme are meant to be read prior to the gathering, though you may want to provide time for the participants to revisit the material or have a leader summarize it in order to help facilitate conversation on the topic.

Be generous with quiet time. Allowing time for the material to "simmer" within each participant may seem like wasted time, but remember that these are not teachings on a theme as much as they are words to guide each individual on a personal journey. We therefore suggest allowing time for people to reflect or journal before beginning any group sharing time.

A WORD ON THE PHOTOGRAPHY

As a "people" photographer, I knew my assignment to do still life photos for this book would be a stretch for me.

One morning as I wandered Chicago looking for images to fit the book's message of transformation, I spotted an open truck packed with recycled cardboard boxes. I had an idea. When the truck stopped at a nearby grocery store, I jumped out and began shooting close-ups of the smashed boxes.

When the driver got out, he spotted me and demanded, "Hey, why are you taking pictures of my truck?" I knew if I stopped, it might involve a long explanation followed by, "Scram!" So I didn't turn my head. I kept shooting and yelled, "It's for a book on women's spirituality."

My non-explanation explanation made me chuckle. I took two or three more frames and then went to talk with him. "You see," I explained, "it's a book about making something new out of the old, about using what's in your life now to make up the next part of your life. They want some photos that show that."

"Oh, I get it," said this middle-aged truck driver. "Then that shot is perfect."

Jean Clough
Evanston, Illinois

Part I

TENDING THE HOLY

Women Giving Birth Together

MIDWIVES OF AN UNNAMED FUTURE

You will know when it is time to bring to birth
the new creation. The signs will be all around you,
urging, insisting: Now is the time.
You have to know just when to bear down
And concentrate on one thing only.
It takes labor, hard, hard labor
to bring to birth something new.

– from "A Psalm for Midwives" by Miriam Therese Winter

Creating Sacred Space

Keep it simple! Place a lighted candle on a table near you, symbolic of your spiritual journey thus far.

Slowing Down

A reading from *Blessings: A WomanChrist Reflection on the Beatitudes* by Christin Lore Weber

The midwife enters the lost places with her who will give birth. The midwife is the woman-between: the liminal woman, the threshold woman. She focuses her energy upon the process of coming through. Coming through birth. Coming through disease. Coming through death. She keeps us breathing, keeps us one with the universal rhythm of creation. She sings the song of breath, turning our fear and the frenetic struggle resulting from it into an intricate dance of becoming. "Behold, the Holy One makes all things new," she reminds. She dances the New Year in; she dances in your soul; she *is* the dance of your soul bringing you through, making you new.

Going Deeper

"May You Walk," a song by Marsie Silvestro (*On the Other Side* album)

> May you walk in the ways of the women who walked before you.
> And may you hear their voices rise — like the wind that gently shakes you.
>
> And know that you are not alone — for we all go with each other.
> Yes, know that you are not alone — as you seek with courage your path.
>
> And may you walk in the ways of the women who went before you.
> And may you feel their laboring hands working to clear the roads you take.
>
> So know that you are not alone — for we all go with each other.
> Yes, know that you are not alone — as your tears push through the pain.
>
> And may you walk in the ways of the women who went before you.
> And may you see that like the rain — they will send deep healing down.
>
> So know that you are not alone — for we all go with each other.
> Yes, know that you are not alone — for your sister's by your side.
>
> As you walk in the ways of the women who went before you
> With the women who are before you — May You Walk.

Reflecting on the Theme

Take a few moments now to linger with the image of a midwife. What is it saying to you about a spirituality for women in times of unprecedented change?

As we women contemplate the profound changes needed in our church and our world these early years of the twenty-first century, it becomes clear that in order to navigate them we need one another more than ever. We must find new ways to stay connected and new images that can sustain us for the work that lies ahead. For not only are we in labor ourselves as we struggle to imagine new ways of moving into the future, but also our relationships with one another are being stretched and challenged as we slowly learn how to join together in this birthing process. It is in this context that we look to the familiar role of a midwife for wisdom that can facilitate what is life-giving within and among us.

The image of a midwife can be traced back to biblical times, where we first read the story of two humble but influential midwives in the Book of Exodus — Shiprah and Puah — whose creativity and fearlessness led them to take on the mighty pharaoh (see Exodus 1:15-21) By working together, these two women were able to ensure the safe birth of the Hebrew children, which eventually led to the exodus of the Hebrew people from their oppressors. Even today their story leaves us with a legacy regarding the power of women's friendships and the courageous paths that have been forged because of them. Perhaps it is this realization and the role of midwife itself that can help us better understand our task and the new ways we are being called to support one another through the unprecedented changes that need to be made in the years ahead.

Women's friendships have empowered women throughout history. Stories from Scripture, such as that of Ruth and Naomi (The Book of Ruth) or Mary and Elizabeth (see Luke 1), often remind us of the impact the presence of another woman has had on our own journey. It is not unusual for us to weave into our conversations the memory of a grandmother, a favorite aunt, a teacher, or a mentor who believed in us, gently guided us at a critical moment in our lives, and left us with pieces of wisdom we continue to cling to today. Though we may not immediately think of these women as "midwives," most of us know the tremendous influence they have had on who we have become. Because of their support, we have launched careers, pursued dreams, taken risks, and some might even say, "come to birth." We know the strength we've found within us when another woman simply stood by our side as we struggled to find our way through miscarriage, divorce, illness, loss, transition, or a variety of other changes in our lives. Like those two wise Hebrew midwives, many of us find creativity and courage in working together that we never would have known if we had been left to confront the pharaoh alone.

In recent years it is often in a circle of women — whether on a retreat, in a book club, at a workshop, or around the kitchen table — that many of us have been helped to make better connections between faith and life, giving birth to a spirituality that is both life-giving and challenging. As we have shared our common concerns and hope for something more, we have begun to uncover new visions of the holy and new experiences of the sacred that have sustained us through some of the roughest times in our personal lives, as well as through times of tremendous upheaval in our church and the world around us.

Wherever we come together as women to deepen our own spirituality, women's stories are told, women's dreams are birthed, and women's conversations pave the way for change. Our heartfelt questions are being articulated over and over again, profoundly challenging all of us to reexamine attitudes and beliefs that have been in place for centuries:

> *"What do I say to my daughter who asks why women can't be priests and cannot even preach on a Sunday?"*
>
> *"Why have we seldom sat in a circle with those from other religious traditions, when our spiritual journeys seem to have so much in common?"*
>
> *"What kind of church do we want for our children and those who will follow us?"*
>
> *"What values from our faith tradition do I want to pass on?"*

While at one time we would have looked to the institutions around us for guidance, today more and more of us are looking to one another. Together we are searching one another out — not so much for answers but for companionship and support as we struggle to free ourselves and the institutions we love from ways of being that are no longer helpful or healthy. Together we are helping one another see new possibilities for the future. In our own way, we are healing, blessing, and sending one another forth to make a difference in the world around us.

Together as women we are embarking on a journey that is profoundly changing our lives as well as our relationships with one another. In small groups and large gatherings, we are helping one another find the courage to stay with chaos, live with uncertainty, clarify what is important, and come to recognize a larger Mystery at work. We are reminding one another that something has ended and something new is trying to emerge. Often we find ourselves telling one another that a new world and a new church needs to be born and that the pain we are feeling is nothing less than the labor pains involved with bringing that unnamed future to birth.

For example, the two of us recently attended a funeral for Sue, a woman we had come to know on a retreat we had given over a year ago. Sitting in the church that morning of the funeral, we witnessed first-hand the power of women's friendships at work — not only accompanying one another in this life but helping a sister in her final great push to cross over to the next. In a Catholic church, with a male priest officiating, women "presided" in a different way: with courage and gentleness and their own lived experience of accompanying a friend from death into life. After Communion, at the request of Sue's family, one of the women described the final gift Sue had given to her friends by inviting them to journey with her throughout the months of her illness. This woman spoke of the many ways Sue's friends had tried to form a circle of support around her. One woman brought Communion to Sue's home each morning; one arranged for meals; one was able to offer massage and healing touch; one made a tape of music that she would play for Sue at different moments of her illness; one supported her as a spiritual companion; one was her nurse. The list of women in Sue's circle went on. While these women all had been Sue's friends over the years, they gradually came to realize that each of them had a specific role in helping to bless the waters of their friend who was in labor, letting go of the life she knew in order to birth a new life. As the two of us listened that day, we understood even more what it means to be a midwife — allowing waters to flow unimpeded from life through death to life again.

In this intimate setting of women telling their stories at the funeral of a friend, a power was released in church that morning. Sue's individual story led to a collective question: Who really presided at this funeral? Those of us who attended certainly got a glimpse of a church that is yet to be — one that recognizes the holiness of ordinary life and acknowledges the creative spirit at work in women's lives. We were all given a glimpse of how women midwife one another, and in the process we were joined together with those early Hebrew midwives as we witnessed the waters of the Exodus separating all over again.

As we women reflect on the ancient art of midwifery, we can begin to glean some of its wisdom and bring it to bear on our relationships with one another and our own role in birthing something new. If the changes we all hope for are ever going to come to birth for our families, our churches, our children, and our world, then we need the supportive presence of spiritual midwives in our midst. We need the lived experience of others as we struggle to stay with the pain, find our way around obstacles, take necessary risks, and let go of old images of who we are and who God is. As midwives to one another, we can remind ourselves when it is time to push and when it is time to breathe deeply and use our energy wisely.

Being a midwife is a cooperative enterprise. When some us are tempted to call the journey off, others are there to remind them that we are all in the process of giving birth and that birth is hard, focused work. Just as the midwife's job is to keep the birthing process holy, so we women must embrace this process of change with reverence, knowing it cannot be rushed. Our job is not to do the work for each other but rather to be there as a reminder that none of us stands alone. The birth of *anything* requires midwives — steadfast encouragers who are there when life seems too great a struggle and birth too hard a process. To midwife the future may very well require defying the status quo: not all that different from what the midwives of biblical times — Shiprah and Puah — had to do. Or it may merely mean that we are there for one another — reminding ourselves to breathe, to trust the process, and to allow a larger Mystery to lead the way.

Honoring Your Experience

▨ Give yourself some time to journal or reflect upon women who have "midwived" you emotionally, professionally, spiritually. How have they made a difference in your life? Name some of the women for whom *you* have been a spiritual midwife (do not forget your daughters, friends, and the daughters of friends).

▨ What challenge does the phrase *midwife of an unnamed future* call to mind for you?

▨ Who or what are the "pharaohs" that you need to beware of as you set about your task?

Reflecting Through Ritual

Let the waters of ordinary life serve as an image of the sacred today. As you turn on the faucet, water a plant, or drink a glass of water — let the experience remind you of a God who is nearer to you than you realize as you help give birth to a future still unnamed.

Moving Back into Daily Life

A prayer from *Autumn Gospel* by Kathleen Fischer

> May the God of Exodus and Emmaus, the God of our seasons and turning points, be with you in this time of transition. May She who is the midwife of change teach you to be gentle with yourself as you let go of the old and await the birth of the new. May She who is the womb of time strengthen you as you cross the river of your own life.

"I Am with You on the Journey," a song by Kathy Sherman, CSJ (*Always With You* album)

> I am with you on the journey, and I will never leave you.
> I am with you on the journey, always with you.

Alternate Ways of Using the Theme with Groups

If you choose to gather in a small group of friends or a large circle, we offer the following suggestions to be adapted to your group's needs and gathering space.

Creating Sacred Space for Your Circle

Place a small table in the center of a circle of chairs. Drape colorful fabric over it and set a lighted candle and small bowl of water upon it, as well as any other symbols that may visually help your group enter into the theme.

Moving Through the Process

Begin the session by asking each person to share why she chose to come to the session and the name of a woman who has midwived her through a challenging time in her life. Then, read the *Slowing Down* reflection and listen to (or sing or read together) the *Going Deeper* song, "May You Walk."

Summarize the *Reflecting on the Theme* or offer people a few moments to look back over the material quietly. Allow time for personal journaling and reflection before beginning a group conversation. You may use the *Honoring Your Experience* questions to launch the conversation and invite each participant to describe her own journey. Or you can begin by simply asking people to share something about the reflection or theme that spoke to them.

A Ritual to Connect You to Daily Life

Read the closing prayer and listen to (or sing or read together) the closing song from *Moving Back into Daily Life*. As the music plays, take the bowl of water from the center and pass it around the circle, inviting each person to bless the woman next to her as the work of birthing the unnamed future continues.

DARING PIONEERS REDEFINING HOLINESS

While it is easier to seek our truth
in the kernel of only one story,
the multi-storied truth, though more elusive,
is a far more wondrous and useful treasure.

– from *River of Courage* by Pam McAllister

Creating Sacred Space

Keep it simple! Bring a favorite book, symbol or photograph that reminds you of women who have influenced your spiritual life to this time of prayer and place it on a table near to you. Light a candle or place fresh flowers nearby if it will help center you.

Slowing Down

A reading from *This River of Courage* by Pam McAllister

> Women's courage is ancient. Wherever there has been slavery, there have been women fighting against slavery. Wherever poor and working people have starved and suffered while the rich danced, there have been women organizing for economic justice. Wherever there has been terror or censorship or the deprivation of basic rights, there have been women daring to raise their voices, lift their hands. These stories have been left out of history books that tell of kings and conquerors, but the continuity of women's courage has forged its own path like water that wears away rock.

Going Deeper

"Standing on the Shoulders," a song by Joyce Johnson Rouse (*Earth Mama: Love Large* album)

I am standing on the shoulders of the ones who came before me.
I am stronger for their courage, I am wiser for their words.
I am lifted by their longing for a fair and brighter future.
I am grateful for their vision, for their toiling on this earth.

We are standing on the shoulders of the ones who came before us.
They are saints and they are humans, they are angels, they are friends.
We can see beyond the struggles and the troubles and the challenge,
When we know that by our efforts things will be better in the end.

Chorus:
They lift me higher than I could ever fly!
Carrying my burdens away.
I imagine our world if they hadn't tried,
We wouldn't be here celebrating today.
We wouldn't be so very blessed today.

I am standing on the shoulders of the ones who came before me.
I am honored by their passion for our liberty.
I will stand a little taller, I will work a little longer.
And my shoulders will be there to hold the ones who follow me.

Reflecting on the Theme

Take a few moments now to reflect on the words to the song "Standing on the Shoulders" and consider how they connect to the theme of this chapter: *Daring Pioneers Redefining Holiness.*

Perhaps the greatest gift of the women's spirituality movement are the amazing stories we tell one another about women who have inspired us to find our own voice and follow our own path. They are often the stories of women who have gone before us: strong women, wise women, women of courage and even defiance. We have stumbled upon them in history books, met them in the pages of Scripture, admired them from afar. And while some of them may not necessarily fit our traditional understanding of holiness, most of us would be quick to include them on the list of holy women whose stories live on in us. These are women who have not only shaped us but have left us a spiritual legacy that might surprise even them.

While some women — such as Rosa Parks on her famous bus ride — have had defining moments in their lives when they risked everything to chart a different course for those who would come after them, other women have quietly gone about leaving a lasting mark on their families and friends for generations to come. Yet all of these heroines found a way to live what they believed. When we reflect on what they endured, it is not surprising that a movie about strong women would be called *Steel Magnolias* or that a book of poetry by Alice Walker would be titled *Revolutionary Petunias*. Clearly, the prevailing stereotypes need to be rethought as we reflect on the real people who "walked the talk" long before the phrase was even part of our vocabulary.

It would seem that these women knew in their bones that we are not given a "cowardly spirit" but one that calls us to be "strong, loving, and wise" (see 2 Timothy1:6-7). They counted on that spirit as they raised families, founded religious communities, confronted those in power, and held on to visions of a church and a world that were yet to be. They were women who persisted in going after what they needed, like the woman in Scripture who pleaded on her daughter's behalf and wouldn't take *no* for an answer (see Matthew 15:21-28) or like Mary Magdalene, who would not allow her own truth to be dismissed as "nonsense" or an "idle tale" (see Mark 16:9-11; Luke 24:1-11).

The more we women tell the stories of these spiritual sages in our lives and history, the more we recognize them not only as women of deep faith but as daring pioneers who have left us with new understandings of what a holy life is all about. They themselves were human, not perfect, and therefore in remembering them we are not left with some unreachable ideal. Instead, we are challenged to be true to ourselves and what we have come to know as the sacred in our own lives.

Part of the spiritual legacy we are left with is their wisdom, which runs through our conversations like a sacred thread connecting one story to another, challenging each of us to treasure our own:

"Listen to your own truth, not to what others say is right or wrong."

"Follow your heart; lean on your inner compass."

"Feel the fear, and do it anyway."

"Trust that there is a part of you that knows the way."

We soon realize there was a part of these women that could not be contained — neither in stereotypes from the past nor in clearly defined roles imposed upon them by their church or the culture at large. As a result, they were often driven by a larger vision that convinced them to push forward — believing in what they could not see and bringing with them a defiant hope that life could be different. This vision became a driving force, a sacred trust that would not allow them to settle in, settle down, or settle for something less than what they knew to be right and just.

The importance of telling the stories of those daring women pioneers and the stories of so many others that are known to only a few was crystallized for Mary Ruth many years ago at an art exhibit by artist Judy Chicago titled *The Dinner Party: A Symbol of Our Heritage*:

As I walked into the room, I was struck first by the tiles on the floor etched with hundreds of women's names. When I looked up, the next scene literally took my breath away. There in front of me was a table with thirty-nine place settings, each with an intricately woven placemat along with a porcelain plate and goblet — all carefully crafted to honor these thirty-nine women, who were clearly representative of so many others and who had never been given a place of honor at any table while they were living. The information gathered to acknowledge the women in the room that day was pieced together from scraps of information that seldom made it into history books. It included the stories of women like Elizabeth and Emily Blackwell, pioneering physicians who established a first-rate medical school for women in 1856; and twelfth century mystic, Hildegard of Bingen, one of the most original thinkers in medieval Europe, an abbess, scientist, scholar, musician, prolific composer, and leading writer of her day. Little by little, these fragments of information were giving me a glimpse of women's accomplishments over time. In experiencing their stories that day, I could palpably feel the price these women had paid, the sin that had been committed in silencing them, and the power that had been unleashed by their finally being honored.

As I look back, I realize that most of the 1,038 women of achievement included at "The Dinner Party" were unfamiliar and their lives and contributions unknown to most of us who attended at that time. But to me it is obvious that this event was meant not only for those women who were being honored but also for the thousands of others who live on in all of us. Clearly, Judy Chicago succeeded in symbolically honoring 5,000 years of women's history in Western Civilization, but her intent was to do even more. It was to remind all women of the importance of our heritage. "All the institutions of our culture tell us through words, deeds, and even worse, silence, that we are insignificant," she wrote. "But in our heritage is our power."

Women's stories need to be told and retold. For too long we have been deprived not only of a collective memory of women's accomplishments but also an understanding of the spiritual fiber they embodied in the struggles and challenges that are now ours. We need to hear their stories and remember our own; but even more we need their passionate faith so we can carry on our own work.

A Japanese poet once wrote, "The world grows stronger as each story is told." Perhaps that is what keeps us telling our stories to one another — stories of ordinary women and those not so ordinary, who have influenced our spiritual lives and are challenging us to embrace new ways of understanding what a holy life is all about. The more we tell our stories, the stronger our connection becomes to that part of ourselves that brings us into relationship with a larger Mystery and a larger Call.

At a time when women's rights was a new and startling concept, Sojourner Truth — a nineteenth century slave — spoke with an inner authority as she set out to abolish slavery and sexism. She relied on a mysterious strength, available to us all as she often claimed, "I talk to God and God talks to me." When Rosa Parks sat down at the front of that Montgomery bus in 1955 and refused to give up her seat, she had no idea what it would spark or what change would result. All she knew was what she had to do. Parks left us with a legacy that goes beyond words: "Be who you say you are, whatever the cost."

Elizabeth Kubler-Ross found herself on the cutting edge of revolutionary change in the medical field by simply asking dying patients what dying felt like. While some members of the scientific community accused her of being a vulture prying on the pain of others, her instincts were telling her how members of the healing profession had yet to embrace death. "I learned to listen to my own gut reaction, not to do what somebody else tells me to do," she wrote. "I learned to follow through when I believe in something and to trust [my gut reaction], no matter how hard it is."

Teresa Kane, a Sister of Mercy, challenged Pope John Paul II while he was visiting the United States in 1979 to give women in the Catholic Church access to all ministries, including ordination to the priesthood. "I had no doubt, no reservations, no deep questions," she reflected, looking back on those four minutes she spent addressing the pope. "I knew it would be controversial, but I knew I had to do it," she said.

These are the kinds of stories we women need to keep telling one another: stories of holy women who heard a call and learned to dance to their own music as a way of following it. At the same time, we also need to keep hearing how women arrived at a place in their lives where the criticism and fear they experienced could no longer shake their own integrity, their sense of being rooted in the sacred, or their confidence that what they were hearing was coming from an authentic experience of the holy. Women who are redefining holiness for us are often those women who came to the edge and found themselves able to fly, only because they were in dialogue with a larger Mystery and a larger Truth.

In her book, *Friends of God and Prophets*, Elizabeth C. Johnson asserts that the symbol of the Communion of Saints needs to "sing again," and she challenges us to not just admire our role models of greatness from afar but also to see them as our companions on the journey and partners in the struggle. Perhaps that is what Judy Chicago did as she compiled her guest list for *The Dinner Party*.

Our spiritual legacy does not lie in the kernel of one story. It is a multi-storied truth about the big and small efforts thousands upon thousands of women have made and are making to bring the sacred feminine to birth once again.

Alice Walker wrote: "I've met Rosa Parks and Fannie Lou Hammer. They have been tempered in the fire of experience and they have come through whole and shining and just to be in their presence is to feel the warmth of their shine." Let these words connect you with the great women you have met in your life. Give yourself time to compile your own guest list, and then let the feast begin. Call to mind those fearless, courageous women whose shoulders you stand upon and whose stories are in your bones. Seat them next to Catherine of Siena, Teresa of Avila, Julian of Norwich, and the other great women saints and mystics from throughout history. Honor them. Bless them. Toast them. Tell them how you are different because of how they lived out their visions and dreams. Listen to what their message is for you today. Feel the warmth of their shine. Then pull up a chair and honor that part of you longing to follow in their footsteps.

Honoring Your Experience

▨ Give yourself time to compile your own "guest list" of women for your own "Dinner Party." Who are the four or five historical women who would have to be invited? Who are the four or five ordinary women you have known who deserve to be honored as well?

▨ Is there a specific woman who has redefined holiness for you? Who is she and how did she do it?

▨ Write a new definition of holiness that speaks to you at this time in your life. What are the key elements that you admire the most? What are the impediments that keep you from practicing this kind of spirituality all the time?

Reflecting Through Ritual

Call to mind a woman who has influenced your spiritual life. As you move through your day, reflect on what her life taught you. Compose a toast to honor her or create a placemat with symbols and words that capture the spirit and the legacy she has left you. At dinner, sit at your dining table, either alone or with others, and toast this woman's life and accomplishments.

Moving Back into Daily Life

A prayer from *In Wisdom's Path* by Jan L. Richardson

God of the generations,
When we set our hands to labor,
Thinking that we work alone,
Remind us that we carry
On our lips
The words of prophets,
In our veins
The blood of martyrs,
In our eyes
The mystics' visions,
In our hands
The strength of thousands.

"Standing Before Us," a song by Carole (Etzler) Eagleheart (*Thirteen Ships* album)

These are the women who throughout the decades
Have led us and helped us to know
Where we have come from and where we are going
Women who helped us to grow.

Standing before us
Making us strong
Lending their wisdom
To help us along
Sharing a vision
Sharing a dream
Touching our thoughts
Touching our lives
Like a deep-flowing stream.

These are the women who joined in the struggle
Angry and gentle and wise
These are the women who called us to action
Who called us to open our eyes.

These are the women who nurtured our spirits
The ones on whom we could depend
These are the women who gave us their courage
Our mentors, our sisters, our friends
These are a few of the women who led us
We know there have been many more
We name but a few
Yet we honor them all
Those women who went on before.

Alternate Ways of Using the Theme with Groups

If you choose to gather in a small group of friends or a large circle, we offer the following suggestions to be adapted to your group's needs and gathering space.

Creating Sacred Space for Your Circle

Set a table for a simple dinner party with a colorful cloth, candlesticks, long taper candles, a vase with flowers. Set one place with a glass to toast collectively all the women who will be remembered and honored in the session. Simple art materials (i.e., construction paper, markers, etc.) can be placed around the space that will be used in a group ritual to design placemats for the women people would like to honor.

Moving Through the Process

Begin the session by inviting each person to share why she came to the session and asking her to name a woman she would like to honor who has influenced their spiritual life. Then, read the *Slowing Down* reflection and listen to (or sing or read together) the *Going Deeper* song, "Standing on the Shoulders." As the group listens to the opening reading and song, have each woman consider the ways the person she mentioned has been a pioneer in redefining her understanding of holiness.

Summarize the *Reflecting on the Theme* or offer people a few moments to look back over the material quietly. Allow time for personal journaling and reflection before beginning a group conversation. You may use the *Honoring Your Experience* questions to launch the conversation and invite each participant to describe her own journey. Or you can begin by simply asking people to share something about the reflection or theme that spoke to them. After the discussion, give participants time and materials to design a place mat — using words, colors, images and symbols — to honor the woman they would like to bring to the feast, providing time for the placemats to be shared and briefly described.

A Ritual to Connect You to Daily Life

Select one person to summarize the sentiments of the session in a toast to all the women honored during this reflection time. Together, raise your glasses of wine or another beverage and recite the following toast before listening to the closing prayer and the closing song from *Moving Back into Daily Life:*

> We lift our glasses to those spirit-filled women who poured out the wine of their lives, their dreams, their prayers, their struggles to show us the way. We take time to remember these and all men and women whose lives were stirred and transformed by a faith in what they could not see; those who became bearers of hope, healing, justice, and peace for us and for our world — sometimes without even knowing it. With many generations we gather in this circle, knowing their journeys made a way for our own. We hold them in our hearts, remember their stories, and invoke the Spirit who stirred their lives to stir ours as well. And we toast them with love and blessing!

> – adapted from *Sacred Journeys* by Jan L. Richardson

PARTNERS IN A PROCESS OF CHANGE

Never doubt that a small group of thoughtful committed citizens
can change the world; indeed, it is the only thing that ever has.

– Margaret Mead

Creating Sacred Space

Keep it simple! Place a lighted candle, small packet of garden seeds, and an ordinary clay pot filled with some dirt on a table next to you.

Slowing Down

A reading from *There Is a Season* by Joan Chittister

> An Arab proverb teaches: *Every morning I turn my face to the wind and scatter my seed. It is not difficult to scatter seeds but it takes courage to go on facing the wind.* The ability to stand steadfast in the face of opposition is the real charism of the sower. The commitment to say a different truth in the face of those who call you liar is the virtue of the sower. The willingness to sow seed on barren ground, on rock, and in thorn bushes is the prophetic task of the sower.

Going Deeper

"Seeds of Change," a song by Carolyn McDade (*Sister Carry On* album)

> This is a time we honor and name those who gathered before us
> This is a time we hear God's word in the voices never heard
> Who shatter all myths of pretension.
> Out of the truth of those turned away, blamed, oppressed and discarded.
> Who shall reap and who shall sow?
> Who decides what seeds will grow,
> and who lays a claim to the harvest?
>
> Chorus:
> Fire of passion, light of vision
> Into the ashes we sow seeds of change
> Rooted a wisdom, dark and fertile
> Yielding a harvest of hope
> Good for all people who live in the land.
>
> Cycles move, people can change,
> Turning fresh in the morning
> Blossoms of joy amidst the pain
> Love that died is born again
> And sacred all lands and all peoples.
> Out of the ash, a cauldron of green
> Fresh, eager and faithful
> Hope long scorned by 'powers that be'
> Lives now as people free
> Their dreams for tomorrow reviving.

Reflecting on the Theme

Have you had the experience of being part of a group working to bring about some kind of change? Think about how that experience changed you.

Since the events of September 11, 2001, the war in Iraq, and Hurricane Katrina, the world seems to be living under a pall of fear and terror. So much of what we women have taken for granted has crumbled or changed; the ripples from those horrific events continue to touch every arena of our daily lives. While acknowledging the critical and even terrifying nature of many of these changes, some of us women believe that this time is not only about endings; and so we look for signs of new life rising from the ashes of all we have lost.

We know that change is not our enemy because so many recent changes are good, even necessary: Women are assuming new roles of leadership, and already we sense they are making a difference; ethics and values are playing an increasing role in the workplace; spirituality and work are no longer mutually exclusive human endeavors.

As we sit with others in spiritual direction or talk together in circles of support, it seems that more and more of us are feeling called to seize *this* moment as the time to sow seeds of change into our many spheres of influence: our workplaces, households, churches, communities, governments, and corporate systems the world over. Most of us already know that sowing and working the soil can be a rigorous, messy enterprise. Yet when we take the time to talk together, we sense the time is right. We keep reminding one another that there is already evidence of new life stirring as women's stories are being told, women's voices are being heard, and the silence of generations is being broken.

Nowhere is this shift more dramatic than in tight-knit corporate corridors, long the province of male power brokers. Recently beset by scandals of monumental proportions, many businesses are suddenly questioning the practices and privileges of the elite few. Ivory towers are crumbling.

Strong and competent women are at the very heart of this upheaval. In several celebrated instances, women first perceived and reported unethical business practices in some of our most prestigious international organizations. Despite enormous pressure to discount and silence them, these women had the inner conviction to stand up and speak out about what they knew to be true, and their courageous words and actions literally had the power to topple corrupt corporate giants.

While it was their voices that captured media attention, these women are a reflection of many other communities of women — some of them ordinary working women, many of them unknown to one another — who over the past few decades challenged basic assumptions about their working environments, authoritarian leadership styles, and the "glass ceiling" that perpetuates women's inferior status and compensation in business, academia, health care systems, politics, and churches.

As the nurturers and sustainers of life, women are often the first to recognize how rigid top-down management styles not only stifle creativity but also ultimately threaten the very life of an organization. These women are keenly aware of the need for dramatic change in our cultural understanding of work. Many are willing to take on backbreaking, heartbreaking, and even spiritbreaking labor to help make such change happen. They know that the task they confront is enormous — and something they can't possibly accomplish alone.

Tapping a natural propensity for relationship, many women are coming together to partner as advocates for more compassionate and empowering working environments. We are banding together in small groups, over lunches or a cup of tea with the hope and intention of transforming the quality of the workplace.

Once each month, some of these women gather during lunchtime in a downtown boardroom to have a focused conversation about integrating their spirituality and their work. The women come from a variety of lifestyles and their work is similarly diverse. What they have in common is their desire to stay in touch with their deepest selves. They make space in their busy schedules because they are *thirsting* to make better connections between what they believe and what they do, between their faith and their work. They know the values they hold near and dear cannot be left at the doorstep when they enter their workplace, because they view all of life as interrelated. For the most part these women speak frankly about wanting their work to be *soulful* — to bring them personal fulfillment and a sense of meaning as well as the opportunity to be stretched and become even more than what they already are. They want to feel passion and zest for their life's work.

These are extraordinary women; they are also real. When they come together each month, they don't hesitate to share their hard stories of trying to balance their personal lives with the demands of their work or their difficulty in trying to stand up and speak out about an array of workplace injustices.

Some carry a weighty feeling of grief over women colleagues who spurn them or compete with them. Indeed, each is aware of the high cost of trying to effect change in her workplace. However, all remain fiercely committed to it, knowing such change can only begin to happen when women can talk together. When they do, these are the kinds of stories they tell:

- a professor cries in outrage for the blatant ageism in her department at the university where she has taught for many years;

- a single mother, trembling, stands up to her boss for his apparent disregard of her personal safety in a job-related incident;

- an executive, her family's primary breadwinner, finds the courage to admit to her spouse the harsh toll her sixty-hour work week is taking on her;

- an entrepreneur reveals her anxiety as she addresses a breach in behavior with her top-ranking employee, who is also a personal friend.

These are snippets of larger and more complex stories, but they illustrate a few of the ways real women, even when so much is at stake, are refusing to compromise themselves or sell their souls. Each woman in the group has admitted that she was able to take a risky stand because she knew she was encircled by other women of integrity from whom she could draw strength and support. She could make the decision to forego approval, or even job security, because she knew she was not alone in holding a vision of a work environment that is both caring and just: a place where one woman's work can become a reflection of her own spirituality and where all employed there have the chance to express their own sacred creativity.

Individually, each of us knows the changes most of us are working toward are small and personal; some are even quite ordinary. Yet it is from sitting in the circle together that we also know the Spirit is always found within and not apart from our ordinary life experience. In our willingness to engage our struggles, to live the passion of our convictions, and to remain faithful to our deepest truth, each person in the circle offers evidence of this Spirit alive — not only within us but also in the work we do.

Could it be that as we partner with one another, *we* become like good seed that, when scattered, has the power not only to transform the culture of the workplace but to change life as well? Indeed, through our conversations, commitment, and courageous actions, it is as if we are collectively giving birth to new paradigms both for living and for working that are already stirring in the ashes we see all around us.

Honoring Your Experience

▦ What does the word *partner* evoke in you? Recall someone who has "partnered" with you in your life and describe what he or she has meant to you.

▦ Is there a situation in your life and work where you can see yourself sowing the seeds of change right now? Describe it in detail: who, what, where, how?

▦ What is your own personal support system? Who helps you water and nurture the seeds of change to fruition? (If you really don't have one, think about where and with whom you might start to develop a "circle of strength.")

Reflecting Through Ritual

Open the packet of seeds and plant them, either outside if the weather will allow or in the pot of dirt. Envision the soil as your workplace or other venue that needs to blossom. As you plant each seed individually, think of different friends, colleagues, church members, or other acquaintances who might give you the strength and support you need to initiate some needed change. When you are done, call up one of the people you thought about and make a date to discuss the issue.

Moving Back into Daily Life

"The House of the Gathering," a poem by May Sarton from *Collected Poems 1930-1993*

> We have been ripening
> to a greater ease,
> learning to accept
> that all hungers cannot be fed,
> that saving the world
> may be a matter
> of sowing a seed
> not overthrowing a tyrant,
> that we do what we can.
>
> The moment of vision,
> the seizure still makes
> its relentless demands:
> Work, Love, Be silent,
> Speak.

"Seeds of Change," a song by Carolyn McDade (*Sister, Carry On* album)

> Chorus:
> Fire of passion, light of vision
> Into the ashes we sow seeds of change.
> Rooting a wisdom, dark and fertile.
> Yielding a harvest of hope
> Good for all people who live in the land.

Alternate Ways of Using the Theme with Groups

If you choose to gather in a small group of friends or a large circle, we offer the following suggestions to be adapted to your group's needs and gathering space.

Creating Sacred Space for Your Circle

Create sacred space for your group as you would for yourself. Dim the lights and gather around a table on which are placed a lighted candle, a small dish of seeds, and an ordinary clay pot filled with some dirt. If the weather allows, meet in a garden or a back yard.

Moving Through the Process

Invite participants to take a few minutes at the beginning of the session to enter the circle of women by sharing what their work — both paid and unpaid — means to them. Then, read the *Slowing Down* reflection and listen to (or sing or read together) the *Going Deeper* song, "Seeds of Change." As the group listens to the opening reading and song, have each woman consider the partners that she has now and has had in the past who gave her strength and support when things needed to be changed in her life.

Summarize the *Reflecting on the Theme* or offer people a few moments to look back over the material quietly. Allow time for personal journaling and reflection before beginning a group conversation. You may use the *Honoring Your Experience* questions to launch the conversation and invite each participant to describe her own journey. Or you can begin by simply asking people to share something about the reflection or theme that spoke to them.

A Ritual to Connect You to Daily Life

At the conclusion of the reflection, pause for a few minutes to allow the material to simmer within you. Invite one woman to the center, take the dish of seeds and pass it around the circle. Have each woman select one seed as a symbol of some change she would be willing to work towards. After each woman names the change in a few words, invite them to place the seed in the pot of dirt. Conclude by listening to the closing prayer and the closing song from *Moving Back into Daily Life.*

Part II

OPENING TO MYSTERY
New Images of the Holy

You can't always change things. Sometimes you don't have no
control over the way things go. Hail ruins crops or fire burns
you out. And then you're just given so much to work with in
a life and you have to do the best you can with what you got.
That's what piecing is. The materials are passed on to you or
are all you can afford to buy…that's just what's given to you…
your fate.

– Mary, a quilter, quoted in
The Quilters: Women and Domestic Art, An Oral History

Creating Sacred Space

Keep it simple! Place a lighted candle and perhaps a few cut squares of fabric on a small table next
to you. If you have a quilt, you can place it nearby or sit with it on you to keep you warm.

Slowing Down

"Fragments," a poem from *Night Visions* by Jan L. Richardson

And so we take the ragged fragments
the patches of darkness
that give shape to the light;
the scraps of desires
unslaked or realized;
the memories of spaces
of blessing, of pain.

And so we gather the scattered pieces
the hopes we carry
fractured or whole;
the struggles of birthing
exhausted, elated;
the places of welcome
that bring healing and life.

And so we lay them at the threshold, God,
bid you hold them, bless them, use them;
ask you to tend them, mend them,
transform them
to keep us warm,
make us whole,
and send us forth.

Going Deeper

"Trouble and Beauty," a song by Carolyn McDade (*This Tough Spun Web* album)

By these laboring wings we have come thus far
to this place in the wind where we see
trouble and beauty
we see trouble, we see beauty
and that far wandering star still calls us on

Chorus:
It's the star will rise and shine
rise and shine
It will rise and shine when earth's
people all are free
It calls to you — it calls to me
Keep your laboring wings till all are free

By this breath conspired we have come thus far
to this place in our song where we sing
trouble and beauty
we sing trouble, we sing beauty
and that far wandering star still calls us on

By these hearts of rage we have come thus far
to this place in our love where we dare
trouble and beauty
we dare trouble, we dare beauty
and that far wandering star still calls us on

By this rainbow, my friends, we have come thus far
to this place in our lives where we live
trouble and beauty
we live trouble, we live beauty
and that far wandering star still calls us on

And this rainbow is you, this rainbow is me
Keep this rainbow, my friends, till all are free

Reflecting on the Theme

Take a few moments now to imagine a patchwork quilt laid out in front of you. Notice both the individual fragments of cloth and the patterns that emerge in the whole.

Long before the term *feminine spirituality* was coined, women were gathering together in one another's homes in a circular configuration around a quilting frame. There they spoke to one another about the issues unfolding in their ordinary lives, even as they were completely engrossed in the work at hand.

Their intention was to craft a quilt, but perhaps gathering with other women was about a whole lot more. The circle might have held a particular lure for the quilters because they knew it as a place where they could come to slow life down, if only for a few hours. It was a place where they could just *be* with the *pieces* of their *own* lives — the joys and pains, the passions and struggles. Maybe this was also the place where they knew they could tap the collective wisdom of the other women present and gain a flash of insight or a glimpse of understanding about a particular issue they were worrying about at the time. One thing this circle surely represented was that they were not alone here in this quilting process. They were held in a grid of support — an awareness that made all the difference.

The quilts the women crafted in this intimate community filled a wide variety of needs. Some were clearly functional and made to provide warmth and protection from the harsh elements; others were like a summary of a family's history, each member represented by a different piece of cloth. Some were quilts made to mark specific celebrations and rites of passage, such as a marriage, the birth of a child, or a significant anniversary. Others would become memorial quilts honoring a loved one recently deceased. There were mammoth quilts and miniature quilts. Each had its particular form and function. Yet there is something about the quilting process itself that speaks to a larger truth and a wider purpose.

Quilting can make great demands on its creators. It requires concentration, discipline, and the commitment to stay with the endeavor over the long haul to completion. A quilter needs vision and imagination to be able to see beyond the random pile of raw materials and to know the relationship of each patch to the whole. The slow, steady, rhythmic motion involved in the sewing of each piece is a constant reminder that quilting cannot be hurried; it takes time and patience, as well as the faith and grace to believe that many disparate fragments can eventually come together into a harmonious whole.

The process is also a uniquely feminine enterprise. At a tender age a young girl is given her *piece bag*, a collection of scraps — calicos, ginghams, velvets and wools — bits and pieces of life deliberately saved and passed on to her as a prelude to joining the circle of quilters. In time she will learn how each woman in the circle is stitching threads of her own life story into this "journal in cloth," teaching her that all of our lives fall to pieces from time to time but that each of us has the power within us to try to stitch it back together again.

Holding history and memory between her fingers, she will come to see how the process itself is all about making connections and forming relationships: connecting women around a quilting frame; bringing different shapes, colors, textures and patterns together into artful compositions; linking past and present by passing quilts down from grandparents to children, from one generation to the next. Much like the women who create them, these quilts become symbols of community, creativity and continuity. There is something about the quilting process — the gathering and storytelling, the piecing and making choices — that says as much about a feminine spirituality as it does about quilting. At the heart of both is the desire to reclaim a vision of wholeness and holiness that is yet to be.

But what does creating a quilt have to do with solving the problems of a depleting earth, a hurting church, or a terror-stricken world? Some would say nothing at all. For those of us engaged in the hands-on work of trying to integrate and reverence all of life, however, quilting seems profoundly connected to a greater purpose.

Let's imagine for a moment the larger quilt of life. It is composed of many disparate pieces, reflective of the many different voices and gifts that are necessary if a new vision of church and society is ever to emerge. Looking at the immensity of the quilt before us, we realize we cannot make every issue confronting us a priority. We each have our own particular piece of the quilt to work on — one small patch that comes out of our own lived experience, out of how the Creator has shaped us through the people and events that have influenced us in our lives thus far.

While some of us are searching for new ways to speak about the sacred, others are daring to name their suffering, hopes, dreams and frustrations — perhaps for the first time. For some of us, our energy is going into personal transformation, while others are propelled by a whole new vision for our aching, hurting world. Still other women are working on the front line to confront systemic injustices.

Indeed, the image of the quilt stands as a compelling metaphor for our own relationship to the whole of creation and how much we need one another on this journey to wholeness. When we listen to each other's stories and tell our own, the quilt begins to take shape. The interplay of patterns offers richness and diversity. Gradually, we begin to see our common threads. Perhaps it is only when we can stand together and embrace our differences that we will begin to grasp the profound connection that unites all of life. Maybe then we will sense how healing our own lives and relationships has an impact that is far-reaching. In a way that is truly mysterious, we might even begin to notice how our personal healing somehow contributes to the mending of our churches, the Earth, and even the world.

For now, the two of us invite you to think of God as a Quilter, the One who wishes to bring all the pieces and patches together. She knows the preciousness and the importance of each ragged square. She knows how in quilting nothing is ever discarded or wasted because everything, even the harsh mismatched piece, has its place and is in fact integral to the overall composition.

Now she hands us the needle and the thread and whispers the following invitation:

> Continue to stitch, my sister,
> be easy with the needle,
> trust the fabric.
> Let the pattern come
> and surprise you, delight you,
> speak to you of visions not yours alone.
> See the visions of all whose lives are in these pieces.
> Touch the peace in each piece.
> You stitch for more than yourself.
> We stitch for more than ourselves.
> We stitch for the world, for the future
> Perhaps we stitch the very heart of God.

– "We Stitch the Very Heart of God" by Juliana Casey, IHM

Honoring Your Experience

What are some of the pieces in your life that still need to be stitched into a larger quilt? Are there several patterns or themes that might encompass them all? What are they?

Is there some part of the quilting process — storytelling, piecing, choosing, connecting — that speaks to you of your "inner work" right now? Explain.

When you image God as a Quilter, are you reminded of anyone in your own life? Who is it, and why does she come to mind?

Reflecting Through Ritual

Take a patch of fabric in your hands. Feel it. Turn it over. Assign a meaning to it from your own life now. Name the piece. During the rest of the day, keep your eyes open for another piece of fabric that might connect in some way with the original piece. When you find it, put them both together in a pouch or a safe place.

Moving Back into Daily Life

"Wholeness," a poem from *I Hear a Seed Growing* by Edwina Gateley

> Gather everything together
> like the enveloping dusk.
> Welcome it,
> delight in it,
> dreams and images,
> memories,
> hopes, pains —
> Recall —
> Relive —
> Befriend.

Let the past surge
forward into the gentle
welcoming present, and
take each
far-wandered memory
into your bosom to kiss,
caress, and
claim your own
your self.

Befriend,
reclaim your wholeness and
all the fragmented beauty of
who you are.

"Trouble and Beauty," a song by Carolyn McDade *(This Tough Spun Web* album)

Chorus:
It's the star will rise and shine
Rise and shine
It will rise and shine when earth's
People all are free.
It calls to you — it calls to me
Keep your laboring wings till all are free.

Alternate Ways of Using the Theme with Groups

If you choose to gather in a small group of friends or a large circle, we offer the following suggestions to be adapted to your group's needs and gathering space.

Creating Sacred Space for Your Circle

Place a patchwork quilt on the floor in the center of a circle of chairs. Set a basket on it with cut squares of fabric, some spools of thread, a pair of scissors, and other quilting supplies inside. As you begin your session, light a candle to illuminate the quilt.

Moving Through the Process

Begin the session by inviting each person to describe her experience with quilts or quilting. If someone has none, encourage her to speak of her impressions of the quilt in the circle. Then read the *Slowing Down* reflection and listen to (or sing or read together) the *Going Deeper* song, "Trouble and Beauty." As the group listens to the opening reading and song, have each woman consider how the various fragments of her life have patterns or themes that can provide a sense of wholeness or holiness.

Summarize the *Reflecting on the Theme* or offer people a few moments to look back over the material quietly. Allow time for personal journaling and reflection before beginning a group conversation. You may use the *Honoring Your Experience* questions to launch the conversation and invite each participant to describe her own journey. Or you can begin by simply asking people to share something about the reflection or theme that spoke to them.

A Ritual to Connect You to Daily Life

Following the group sharing time, take the basket of quilting supplies and pass it around the circle, inviting each woman to choose one of the cut fabric squares to remind her that in quilting *every* piece has its place, nothing is wasted, and everything belongs; the same is true about the pieces of our lives. Invite each woman to share why she chose the piece she did. Conclude by listening to the closing prayer from *Moving Back into Daily Life* and singing (or reading together) the chorus to the song "Trouble and Beauty."

SPINNING A FINELY TEXTURED LIFE

> Each morning I have seen
> how her agile fingers
> choose the thread
> one by one.
>
> – Julia Esquivel

Creating Sacred Space

Keep it simple! Place a lighted candle and a few strands of yarn on the table next to you as a way of reminding you that your life is an unfolding tapestry.

Slowing Down

"Spinningwoman God," a poem from *Lifelines: Threads of Grace Through Seasons of Change* by Alla Renée Bozarth

> Whole-unto-Herself
> but needing us,
> She busies Herself
> with the universe —
>
> Her cosmos is more
> than cosmetic.
> She needs to touch,
> hold, and listen, so

She gives birth
to a creation
needing to be
touched, held, and heard.

Her body the spindle shank
of spun light, we Her spun gold,
Her opening gyre, Her choreography
of Grace — Spinner God unwinds
Herself into creation, a fiery twirl,
a twirling fire, a circle dance,
She dances the round with us,
forming her favorite shapes
in a rounding motion,
an open embrace….

She Who Is
    gracious
She Who Is
    friendly
She Who Is
    becoming

Befriends us anew
with each turn of Her spool,
befriending all beings
with the dance of Her hand,
playing music with Her spheres,
and weaving complexities,
infinities, and making braids.

Going Deeper

"I Am a Weaver Woman," a song by Marsie Silvestro (*Crossing the Lines* album)

Chorus:
I'm weaving…I'm a weaver
I'm weaving…I'm a woman
I'm a woman…I'm a weaver
I'm a weaver…I'm a woman

And I am a woman weaver
Pulling all the threads
Weaving the names of women
Voices in my head.

And I shuttle out their wisdom
And I gather all their grace
As I unravel here before me
This woman-loving lace.

And I am a woman weaver
Pulling all the threads
Weaving the pain of women
Some now living, some now dead.

And I shuttle out their teardrops
And I latchloop all their cries
As I entwine the pain of struggle
Colored patterns tell me why.

Reflecting on the Theme

Take a few moments now to imagine yourself sitting at a spinning wheel, working with the many threads of your own life.

God is mystery. How often are we all reminded of that! How challenging it can be to let God be God and allow ourselves to hold many images of the holy over a lifetime, knowing they are all inadequate. As we take up the quilt of our own lives or imagine ourselves sitting at a spinning wheel, there are new images of the sacred that will be there to accompany us if we are open to receiving them. They are not necessarily there to take the place of how we have imaged God from the beginning, but they can companion us as we embrace the task of spinning a finely textured life. Together, these many images have a way of introducing us to the feminine face of God — if we have not met her before. Each has the power to lead us back into a larger Mystery that no one image is able to contain.

As we set out to reflect on what it might mean to spin a finely textured life, take a moment to imagine God as a Spinningwoman sitting at the wheel with us, making the sacred thread that connects all the various pieces of life we are holding at this time. As we linger with her, she may take on the face of a mother, a grandmother, a friend, a mentor. Regardless of how we see her, she is a powerful presence in our midst. As she pulls the threads that turn the spinning wheel, we get a sense that she knows better than anyone else what is involved in the hard work of spinning a finely textured life. Like a quilter, she wants us to sit by her side and learn the craft.

Some claim that this Spinningwoman God knows "circle work" better than anyone else. In fact, long ago she fell in love with circles — with all that is round and all that goes around. She invites us to do the same: reminding us of the Native American Circle of Stones that provides a sacred space for the Vision Quest; the Medicine Wheel that carries healing energy; the Labyrinth that keeps us on a sacred path; the Potter's Wheel that is as much about centering ourselves as it is about centering a pot. She has known all along that life is not lived on a straight line. Life is not a series of events progressing in a linear way from beginning to end, from birth to death. She wants us to know that the wheel keeps turning, that life is a circle; and she reminds us often that the life/death/life cycle — the paschal mystery as we experience it over a lifetime — needs to be honored.

Spinningwoman God teaches us that our lives are ordered by circular movement. We all share the same spinning earth. We greet the same sun. We experience recurring seasons and cycles. There is a rhythm to things. When we realize this, change becomes the norm and stability is recognized as an illusion.

Spinningwoman God keeps reminding us that we all go around the wheel many times in life, learning and re-learning the same lessons that spinners and spiritual seekers before us have done. In fact, as we sit at her feet, we begin to hear this age-old wisdom once again:

> "*You begin to spin by spinning.*"
>
> "*You can learn to spin anything, even lint from the dryer or grief from the loss of a loved one; nothing is meant to be wasted.*"
>
> "*You begin with what you have at hand, the threads of your daily life.*"
>
> "*You must practice spinning: sitting still, slowing down, and finding your own rhythm as you work with the treadle.*"
>
> "*Work with all the colors that come your way, those that are strong and vibrant and those that are resistant to being woven in.*"

We soon realize that spinning a finely textured life is a process that takes a lifetime, and the skills we need are not all that different from what we can learn as we use our imaginations and sit quietly with our Spinningwoman God. It is there that we are reminded of how these feminine arts — these repetitive rhythms — have always had a way of leading people to the center of themselves. More often than not, they have freed many of us to become channels of creativity and imagination in our families, churches, and the world we are a part of.

Step by step, we take an early morning walk. Day by day, we write in a journal, work in a garden, light a candle, return to a piece of poetry, or go about the everyday things that keep life going. It all seems so slow, so ordinary. Still, thread by thread, we are learning the importance of staying faithful to a process and reminded that there is no way to cultivate our souls in a hurry. There is no way to rush healing, forgiving, grieving, even growing; it is all about the slow process of transformation.

May Sarton reminds us: "Solitude cracks open the inner life/silence nourishes us like food for the soul." It shouldn't surprise us, then, to hear that sitting at a spinning wheel is not only about producing beautiful cloth but also about cracking open the inner life of the spinner in the process. How often have we as women come to realize that we are not going to be the same person after we thread our way through loss, change, transition. How often have we had to learn and relearn that the design will emerge in the process and that the outcome is not for us to know. Phyllis Tickle says it this way in her book *My Father's Prayer:* "Mainly the coverlet showed me that Mama was right. Stitches do take the time they are made in and spend it to change the people who are making them…. Watch the people as much as their stitches."

As we watch, we learn from others. We especially learn from those who have stayed at the loom of their own lives and followed that inner thread all the way around — through life, death, and life again. Some of them we rub shoulders with every day; others inspire us from a distance. All of them have created tapestries that provide a model for our own.

Mahatma Gandhi was convinced of the calming, meditative effect of spinning and made it a point to spin daily. As the industrial world flooded into India, Gandhi urged each Indian to spend time at his or her spinning wheel daily. He saw it as both a practical activity and a spiritual discipline. Some say it was his way of connecting with ordinary people. Others claim it was the simple and repetitive rhythm that helped him cope with the stresses of life. Perhaps Gandhi wanted the Indians themselves to spin their nation into peace and healing. Whatever it was, it calls our attention to the mystical process available to us as we enter into any kind of repetitive spiritual practice, whether it be walking, sitting, meditating, praying, quilting or spinning. "Watch the people as much as their stitches," says Phyllis Tickle. As we do, we begin to see how they are being changed in the process.

Continuing to spin a finely textured life, we realize how much we learn with our hands, as well as from our mistakes and the example of those who are further along on the road. We especially learn from the women poets, mystics, and prophets who have gone before us: Hildegarde of Bingen, Julian of Norwich, Teresa of Avila, Catherine of Siena, Rosa Parks, Elizabeth Cady Stanton, Georgia O'Keefe, May Sarton — each weavers and spinners in their own way. We begin to connect with women like these who brought to birth a new reality from their own experience — a woman's experience.

How did they do it? They simply followed a thread and made connections that others weren't making. Their lives talked about circles and the earth and a God who was mother as well as father. They lived life with passion, knowing they needed to pass on a better world to their children and grandchildren, to future generations. Sometimes they were silenced; often they were ignored. Yet step by step they continued to spin a finely textured life, and their memory challenges us to do the same.

There is obviously still a long way to go, but the spinning wheel is turning. Women are spinning new threads out of their own life experience. Not only are individuals befriending change but also a whole paradigm shift is underway. One whole way of seeing life, which has been in place for 5,000 years, is beginning to give way to another. It is about making room for the feminine. It is about the interwoven quality of all of life and bringing together what has been separated. It is about trusting our own experience of the sacred, even the woven quality of our struggles, and coming to see that racism, sexism, ageism, and homophobia are all interrelated.

Finally, as women we are seeing ourselves as connected not only to one another but to the Earth as well. We are seeing more clearly how intertwined our lives are with all of creation. We are giving voice to the words of Chief Seattle that continue to ring true for us: "What we do to the earth, we do to ourselves." These truths are getting into our bones and taking root around the world. And the wheel continues to turn.

It comes as no surprise to those of us who are in the process of giving birth to something new that transformation and change come with a cost. Jesus knew it 2,000 years ago, and we are still learning it today. He was crucified because he was challenging the institutions of his day, questioning the status quo and the powers that be. Jesus was not afraid to pay a steep price to see a new world come to fruition.

To see life as a tapestry and to spin a finely textured life is upsetting to the world order that has been taken for granted for centuries. However, we are not left alone at the wheel. The ancient weaver lives in our souls. She spins the thread for our diapers and our shrouds; she keeps us aware that everything is connected. She reminds us that the Holy is in our midst and woven into the fabric of life itself. Over and over again, she points out that we are part of a larger tapestry, weaving not only for ourselves but also for a future we may never see.

We invite you to bring your own tapestry to prayer. Sit at the feet of the Spinningwoman God, give yourself time to learn what she has to teach about this birthing process, and then in small ways give yourself time to share with others what you have come to learn.

Honoring Your Experience

▦ Describe the frayed threads in your life's tapestry. Now hold them up with love and care. Look at them fondly. What do they teach you?

▦ As you sit with the tapestry of your own life, what are some new threads you think you need at this time? How are you going to spin them?

▦ Name a time when you had to let go of the tapestry of your life that you wanted to weave. Tell how the pattern had to change as you worked with a relationship, your career, a piece of your spiritual journey, a life dream.

Reflecting Through Ritual

Take a piece of yarn and put it in your pocket or purse. Each time you run across it, remind yourself that the tapestry of your life continues to unfold. When you discover the perfect place, tie the yarn to it as a way of making a connection with the ancient weaver who keeps sitting at the spinning wheel of your life.

Moving Back into Daily Life

A reading from Deena Metzger in *Weavings* magazine

> Each day is a tapestry. Threads of broccoli, promotion, couches, politics, shopping, building, planting, thinking interweave in intimate connection with insistent cycles of birth, existence, and death. We can become so focused on our accomplishments that we will not even see the holy, sacred, healing grace of God present all around us as we travel.

"Indian Tapestry," an excerpt from *Threatened with Resurrection,* a poem by Julia Esquivel

When I go up to the House of the Old Weaver,
I watch in admiration
What comes forth from her mind:
A thousand designs being created
And not a single model from which to copy
The marvelous cloth
With which she will dress
The Companion of the True and Faithful One.

Men always ask me
To give the name of the label,
To specify the maker of the design.
But the Weaver cannot be pinned down
By designs,
Nor patterns.
All of her weavings
Are originals,
There are no repeated patterns.

Her mind is beyond
All foresight.
Her able hands do not accept
Patterns or models.
Whatever comes forth, comes forth,
But she Who is will make it.

The colors of her threads
Are firm:
Blood,
Sweat,
Perseverance,
Tears,

Struggle,
And hope.
Colors that do not fade
With time.

The children of the children
Of our children
Will recognize the seal
Of the old weaver.

Maybe then it will be named.
But as a model,
It can never again
Be repeated.

Each morning I have seen
How her agile fingers
Choose the threads
One by one.

Her loom makes no noise,
And men
Give it no importance,
And nevertheless,
The design
That emerges from Her Mind
Hour after hour
Will appear in threads
Of many colors,
In figures and symbols
Which no one, ever again,
Will be able to erase
Or undo.

"We Are the Weavers," a song by Marsie Silvestro (*Crossing the Lines* album)

Chorus:
We are the weavers of life and of love
Pullin' the threads of our stories in and out.

Blue thread for water rising.
Green threads, we bring peace.
Yellow, for the line of horizon.
And Orange fires us on.
Yes, Orange fires us on.

Red threads, for the love sweet lovin'.
Purple, passion's deep.
Black threads, for the faces shining.
And Brown for our roots in the earth.
Brown for our roots in the earth.

Alternate Ways of Using the Theme with Groups

If you choose to gather in a small group of friends or a large circle, we offer the following suggestions to be adapted to your group's needs and gathering space.

Creating Sacred Space for Your Circle

Gather chairs around a spinning wheel. If one is not available, use a picture of one. Place a piece of colorful fabric, a lighted candle, and baskets of yarn at the base of the wheel.

Moving Through the Process

Begin the session by asking participants to imagine themselves spinning the wheel. Have each person choose a piece of yarn from the basket and keep it wrapped around their hand during the session. Then read the *Slowing Down* reflection and listen to (or sing or read together) the *Going Deeper* song, "I Am a Weaver Woman." As the group listens to the opening reading and song, have each woman reflect on the piece or pieces she is trying to weave into the tapestry of her life at this time.

Summarize the *Reflecting on the Theme* or offer people a few moments to look back over the material quietly. Allow time for personal journaling and reflection before beginning a group conversation. You may use the *Honoring Your Experience* questions to launch the conversation and invite each participant to describe her own journey. Or you can begin by simply asking people to share something about the reflection or theme that spoke to them.

A Ritual to Connect You to Daily Life

Following the group sharing time, invite participants to bring the strand of yarn they chose at the beginning and stand in a circle around the baskets and the spinning wheel. Conclude by listening to the closing prayer from *Moving Back into Daily Life* and listening to (or singing or reading together) the song "We Are the Weavers." As people leave, suggest they take the strand in their hand with them as a reminder that the tapestry of their life continues to unfold. Have them find a place in their home where they can tie the string or yarn as a way of making a connection with the ancient weaver who continues to work with them to spin for themselves a finely textured life.

BECOMING BREAD

Blessed are you, O God,
who brings forth the bread of faith
from the earth.
Like the yeast by which a bakerwoman
leavens the whole loaf,
our companionship with you
passes down from generation
to generation.

– from *Sacred Journeys* by Jan L. Richardson

Creating Sacred Space

Keep it simple! Place a lighted candle and a small packet of dry yeast on a table next to you.

Slowing Down

"Blessing the Bread: A Litany" from *Our Passion for Justice* by Carter Hayward

Then, God, gathering up
    her courage in love, said:
"Let there be bread!"

And God's sisters
Her friends and lovers
Knelt on the earth
Planted the seeds
Prayed for the rain
Sang for the grain
Made the harvest
Cracked the wheat
Pounded the corn
Kneaded the dough
Kindled the fire
Filled the air
With the smell of fresh bread
And there was bread!
And it was good!

We the sisters of God say today,
All shall eat of the bread,
and the power.
We say today,
All shall have power
And bread.

Today we say,
Let there be bread!
Let there be power!
Let us eat of the bread
And the power!
And all will be filled
For the bread is rising!

Going Deeper

"Holy Bread," a song by Ida Gannon *(unpublished)*

Holy bread, holy people
Holy space, blessed time in our lives
Sharing our laughter
Sharing our pain
Telling our stories
Proclaiming our name.

Holy Wisdom, gather and blend
Mix and bake, knead and shape.
Bond us together
North and South
East and West
We're strengthened
We are blessed.

Many grains, many colors
Many tables, all make one bread.
Many signs, many symbols,
Many spirits
Proclaiming our dreams.

Reflecting on the Theme

Take a few moments with a piece of fresh bread, either real or imaginary. Smell it. Feel it. Eat it. Imagine becoming bread for others.

Baking bread from scratch can be an invitation to experience wonder. Simple ingredients, crushed and dried, are transformed before our eyes into a substance that is both fragrant and life-giving. In fact, bread making is a lot like soul work: Both require slow, repetitive, hands-on attention that cannot be controlled or hurried. Both are hard work, and each can be undertaken only when the conditions are right.

Bread is a powerful metaphor on so many levels and in many faith traditions. Perhaps it is because bread taps into a universal need to be fed and nourished. Centuries ago, Jesus called his friends together around a table and gave them bread as a way to remember him and become one with him. Today, you are invited to gather with us around the table of ordinary life and allow bread to become our teacher.

There is a line in Scripture that reads: "The kingdom of heaven is like yeast that a woman took and mixed in with three measures of flour until all of it was leavened" (Matthew 13:33). In this excerpt God is being compared to a woman making bread — a Bakerwoman God! This Bakerwoman God is a hands-on God, one who is at home in the kitchen. She knows the wisdom of holding, forming, and kneading until the dough is just the right shape, and ideal texture. This Bakerwoman God knows that *becoming* is ongoing, so she stays present to the moment — her focus not on completion or on the finished product but on the process itself. She knows that the bread will rise in its own time, just as our own inner lives will unfold gradually and in a timely manner.

Bakerwoman God knows that women of substance, like bread, are works in progress. Her altar is the kitchen table, and on it she displays the sacred elements: flour, water, honey, oil, salt and yeast — all the staples necessary to create a fine loaf of bread. Here she reminds us how each of these ingredients corresponds to some quality in us. For example, the wheat might be compared to the "grains of experience" that have been ground down by our loves and losses, our joys and pains, our daily dyings and risings. Water, which softens the dough and keeps it from becoming coarse, might compare to the waters of our lives: our tears, our breath, our blood. Salt is a flavor enhancer and a preservative. It can be a stirring metaphor for that part of us that is earthy and authentic. Honey and spices sweeten the bread and serve as the activating agents for the yeast. A loaf of bread becomes a unique creation with the choice of sweetener and spices. Butter or oil contribute to the bread's texture and tenderness and suggest resiliency — a quality that is so essential if we are to make the long and arduous journey to becoming women of substance.

The final element, the yeast, is the leavening — the mystery ingredient, the symbol of both potential and possibility. Yeast is that part that helps the dough — and us — rise. As we observe the staples sitting before us, we undoubtedly realize that we have everything right here to create a fine loaf of bread. Do we also recognize that we already have within *us* everything we need for our own becoming?

Too often, we focus on that part of us that we believe is "not enough." We receive messages from our culture and even from our faith traditions that reinforce our fear that we are inadequate, lacking in essentials, not quite "measuring up." In our efforts to become perfect as our God in heaven is perfect (see Matthew 5:48), we tend to strive for some ideal of perfection outside of ourselves.

Bakerwoman God invites us to look within and to focus on the yeast. She reassures us that rising happens from the inside out, if we are open to it. Yeast is the activating agent in each of our lives — that part of us that knows how to rise up out of all that tries to hold us down. It is the spark of divinity, the Spirit within us that can do infinitely more than we could ask or imagine (see Ephesians 3:20). The yeast takes us by surprise and helps us to see that we are more than what we seem to be; we are, indeed, good enough. Our only task is to make room for this mystery and allow it to do its work. Like the yeast rising slowly in the bread dough before us, we become women of substance over time by allowing ourselves to journey to that sacred region deep within us where transformation can take place. This is where our priorities and values get clarified, where courage and fresh vision are reclaimed. But like bread making, this is not a process without toil.

Just as mystery starts to take shape and the bread begins to rise, the baker knows it is time to punch down the dough by literally thrusting a fist into the light fluffy mass already overflowing the mixing bowl. Punching down releases the gases and toxins that accumulate during the rising process and prevents the dough from becoming tough and untextured. Though necessary, this step — as well as the kneading and pushing and shaping that follow — can seem harsh, even violent at times. But as we linger with these difficult images they can begin to speak to us of the inevitability of suffering and the high cost involved in change.

Wouldn't we all like to embrace a life devoid of suffering? Wouldn't we like to believe that becoming women of truth, depth, and integrity would be rewarded in kind? Yet frequently, the opposite is true. To embark on this type of journey is, in many ways, to follow the "road less traveled," as M. Scott Peck called it. Often much is asked of us, sometimes even more than we feel capable of surviving. Loss, the death of a loved one, illness, divorce, family struggles, betrayals — experiences like these can leave us feeling not only punched down but at the same time pulled and stretched and even flattened beyond what we feel we can possibly endure.

Again the bread continues to be an instructive metaphor. Once it has been punched all the way down, a cloth is placed over the mixing bowl so that a second rising can take place in the dark. This is not unlike the experience of suffering, which some religious traditions describe as the "dark night." As we pause at the mixing bowl to observe the effect of the second rising, our perspective on the power of the darkness may begin to shift. What formerly seemed menacing and even frightening may, if we can stay with it, become a harbinger of a deepening dimension of our faith. As we are being stretched and shaped, we may begin to move beyond an image of a God who *causes* suffering to an awareness that suffering itself is steeped with the *presence* of God. "When order crumbles, mystery rises," says theologian John Shea. Maybe it is only as we are pushed to our own limits — punched down, kneaded and stretched beyond our comfort zone — that we can finally begin to yield and become like dough in the warm and capable hands of our Bakerwoman God. She is the one who holds and caresses us during difficult times. She helps us rise and promises to be with us no matter what the conditions of our lives.

Certainly just staying with the image of bread making will not provide an answer to the question, "Why must we suffer?" However, as we linger with the question we might discover how frequently through suffering we come to know that our lives are not lived for ourselves alone. The story of bread is about life, death, and rising again to new life. This is our story too. As women of substance we may begin to understand that our lives are far richer than we may have imagined. The process of daily living has a way of shaping us, deepening our spirituality, and bringing us into contact with a God who is closer than we realize. As women of substance we may come to realize that, much like bread, life has to be worked with and worked through. Like bread, we too are meant to rise.

Honoring Your Experience

🔲 Name a bread maker you have known. Describe how she went about the work of making bread. What were the qualities that you most remember or admire about her?

🔲 Is there a particular part of the bread making process — mixing, rising, kneading, baking, cooling — that connects to an aspect of your life experience at this time?

🔲 Does the image of yeast help you deal with some of the difficulties of your life? How so?

Reflecting Through Ritual

Take your packet of yeast. Open it. Pour it into a cup of warm water. Touch some of the mixture to your tongue. Let it remind you of the Mystery you carry within you at all times.

Moving Back into Daily Life

"The Rising of the Loaf," a poem by Susan F. Jarek-Glidden from *Wellsprings: A Journal for United Methodist Women*

"It takes lots of time," the Grandmother said,
"It takes lots of time to make health-full, whole bread.
You work from the dawning past the set of the sun,
But the rising of the loaf isn't done, isn't done—
The rising of the loaf isn't done."

"It takes lots of time," the strong Mother said,
"It takes lots of time to make holy bread.
You think you've finished, but you've hardly begun,
For the rising of the loaf isn't done, isn't done —
The rising of the loaf isn't done."

"It takes lots of time," the wise Daughter said,
"It takes lots of time to make new bread.
For when it's completed, a new song will be sung,
But the rising of the loaf isn't done, isn't done —
The rising of the loaf isn't done."

"It takes lots of time," the Three said with one voice,
"But when the loaf's risen, we all will rejoice.
And we'll know what we've started has truly begun,
For the rising of the loaf will be done, will be done,
For the rising of the loaf will be done."

"See Me How I Rise," a song by Marsie Silvestro (*Circling Free* album)

Chorus:
See me how I rise,
No more tears in my eyes,
See me I'm standing oh so strong,
I am a woman…
I am a woman…
And I've come to sing, come to sing my song.

And I will restore you,
And heal your wounds again,
And you will shine as sunshine does
After it's blessed the rain.

Then I will
Wipe your tears dry,
And sorrow will be gone,
And you will sing a new melody,
And I will be your song.

Alternate Ways of Using the Theme with Groups

If you choose to gather in a small group of friends or a large circle, we offer the following suggestions to be adapted to your group's needs and gathering space.

Creating Sacred Space for Your Circle

Place an ordinary kitchen cloth over a table at the center of a circle of chairs in your gathering space. Display a large mixing bowl, a lighted candle, an opened package of baking flour, a pitcher of water, some oil, a jar of honey, a salt shaker, and a basket containing several packets of dry yeast.

Moving Through the Process

Begin the session by inviting each participant to tell about a woman who was a bread maker. Then read the *Slowing Down* reflection and listen to (or sing or read together) the *Going Deeper* song, "Holy Bread." As the group listens to the opening reading and song, have each woman consider the role that bread has played in their own lives.

Summarize the *Reflecting on the Theme* or offer people a few moments to look back over the material quietly. Allow time for personal journaling and reflection before beginning a group conversation. You may use the *Honoring Your Experience* questions to launch the conversation and invite each participant to describe her own journey. Or you can begin by simply asking people to share something about the reflection or theme that spoke to them.

A Ritual to Connect You to Daily Life

Before the session begins, gather around a kitchen table where one person has already mixed together the ingredients for a loaf of bread. Invite each person to take a turn performing one part of the breadmaking process — punching down the dough, kneading it, shaping it — before placing the bread in the oven to bake. After the *Moving Through the Process* discussion, gather at a kitchen table to eat the bread! Each participant may choose to extend her hand in silent blessing over the warm bread while one person breaks it open and shares it around the table. Conclude by listening to the closing prayer from *Moving Back into Daily Life* and singing (or reading together) the song "See Me How I Rise." As an alternative, end by reading together the poem on the next page:

"Even Crumbs Are Bread" a poem from *Becoming Bread* by Gunilla Norris

Be careful with the crumbs.
Do not overlook them.

Be careful with the crumbs:
The little chances to love,

The tiny gestures, the morsels
That feed, the minims.

Take care of the crumbs:
A look, a laugh, a smile,

A teardrop, an open hand. Take care
Of the crumbs. They are food also.

Do not let them fall.
Gather them. Cherish them.

Part III

KNOWING WHEN TO PUSH
Trusting a New Vision

CROSSROADS AND THRESHOLDS

As we stand on such thresholds, life itself is commissioning us
to move onto a new stage of our Becoming. Something at the
core of our being is urging us forward…as surely as the onset
of labor pain and the breaking of the waters commission the
expectant mother to begin the process of birthing.

– from *Sacred Spaces* by Margaret Silf

Creating Sacred Spaces
Keep it simple! Place a lighted candle and some object from nature (a seashell, a stone, a feather) as
a symbol of Native American spirituality on a table next to you.

Slowing Down
A reading adapted from Habakkuk 2:2-4

Write down the vision
clearly upon the tablets,
so that one can read it readily.
For the vision still has its time,
presses on to fulfillment,
and will not disappoint;
if it delays, wait for it.
It will surely come,
it will not be late.

Going Deeper

"Gather the Dreamers," a song by Kathy Sherman, CSJ (*Gather the Dreamers* album)

Gather the dreamers and wake the sleeping,
now is the time to give birth to the dream.
Gather the dreamers, a new day is dawning,
the time is now and the earth is calling our name.

Gather the lovers and heal the broken,
weave all the earth with heartstrings of love.
Gather the lovers, a new day is dawning,
the time is now and the earth is calling our name.

Carried within us, a dream,
dare we grasp now the moment.
We can make dreams come true
if our vision is new.
It's a quest that belongs to us all.

Peacemakers gather and teach forgiveness,
link hands through all lands in a circle of peace.
Peacemakers gather, a new day is dawning,
the time is now and the earth is calling our name.

Reflecting on the Theme

Take a few minutes to journal or think about a time of threshold in your own life. What are the transitions that you are currently facing?

Change is difficult; it is made more so by a society that prizes security and rewards stability. Indeed, many people in our western culture look upon sudden or unexpected change as something to be avoided, a disgrace of some kind, or even the failure to manage one's life well. Is it any wonder, then, that many of us recoil in self-doubt when something interrupts the familiar pattern of our lives or when we find ourselves staring into the face of the unforeseen?

Such an experience can be precipitated by a "life accident" — the sudden onset of an illness, the death or betrayal of a loved one, even the loss of a job or of a lifestyle that we have enjoyed and found fulfilling. Other times, the interruption may be subtle and come from within us. It can arrive as a pervasive restlessness, loneliness, or feeling of malaise that is difficult to explain or describe. All we know is that something deep beneath the surface of who we are has shifted. We are in pain; something is cramping our soul.

These disquieting experiences are "threshold moments," explains mythologist Joseph Campbell, times when "the familiar life horizon has been outgrown, when the old concepts, ideals and emotional patterns no longer fit" who we are. Campbell's words are wise and poetic, but practically speaking, when we think of those times when our own life has been turned upside down, we want to groan over the huge knot in the pit of our stomach. Each of us will experience it in our own way, of course, but threshold moments almost always usher in a period of personal upheaval and a time of deep soul-searching. One way of life has ended, and we are adrift. We are no longer where we once belonged and felt comfortable; we now stand at the edge of the unknown.

As women who have navigated such uncertain times, we use words like *anxious, alone, confused,* and *afraid* to describe our feelings in the midst of transition. Some of us prefer metaphors: *standing at the crossroads, reaching a point of no return, moving through a thick fog of anxiety,* or *being thrust onto a precipice overlooking an abyss.* All suggest that our crossroads and thresholds are tumultuous times when we must say goodbye to what we have known and loved, then sit and wait awhile before we are able to move on. For most of us, this happens many times over the course of our lives.

Our birth was our first transition. Before we were born, our mother's womb was the only life we knew, a place where we were safe and secure from all intrusions. That security was shattered abruptly, however, as we were pushed through the dark space of the birth canal, our new life about to begin.

Thresholds are the dark spaces, the time "in between." Like childbirth, entering into this "in-between time" can demand a great deal from us. Those of us who have given birth — or have witnessed it — know that it can be extremely painful. We need all the courage we can muster to let go of what needs to be left behind and to surrender to that which feels completely alien to us. While it is certainly tempting to focus only on the discomfort in times of transition, staying with the birth metaphor can help us remember that the pain and the pushing are just one part of a much larger process. It challenges us to trust that all is not lost if we can stay open to the new life that is trying to break through.

Trusting and staying open are difficult enough, but living through the gap of time "in between" can also undermine our sense of security. Jungian analyst Marion Woodman calls this transitional time "the twilight zone," where one part of us is "looking back, yearning for the magic we have lost" while another part looks ahead with excitement for some "changing potential." Back and forth, betwixt and between — little in our culture offers us support or prepares us for such ambiguity and confusion. Those around us, even loved ones, can grow impatient with our discomfort and might advise us to "get on with life" or to leap immediately into a new way of living, without any regard for the psychological and spiritual importance of this time "in between."

A feminine spirituality, on the other hand, invites us to expand our vision and to look to traditions and cultures outside our own as a way of gaining new insight or a broader perspective on how to stay faithful to the mystery unfolding within us, while simultaneously preparing us to navigate our way through difficult times.

Many indigenous cultures, such as that of the Celts and the Native Americans, see change not as some isolated moment of existence but as the very pattern of all life. Their rituals and rites of passage help them grasp that a time of transition, while sometimes seen as perilous, can actually be a holy passage and a rich opportunity for new growth in their lives. One widely-recognized ritual used to mark transitional events among Native Americans is the Vision Quest, a process that encourages people to pause and create some sacred time and space in order to reconnect to a deeper part of themselves and help unfurl a vision for their lives. It is a ritual, we believe, that has much to offer us as we make our own journey through the unknown.

For example, the first stage of the Vision Quest can feel radical to a beginner, because the primary task is to separate from one's familiar surroundings. A Native American will move to a remote place, into what he or she might call the "wilderness," and mark off with a circle of stones a sacred space in which to dwell for the duration of the ritual process, usually a minimum of three days. Often with only water for sustenance, he or she will sit alone in this space to invoke the Great Spirit.

Our own times of turmoil frequently compel us to step out of routine and away from all the distractions in our lives. This could be a time when busyness or the hurried pace of life leaves us feeling depleted, times when we yearn for some solitude to heal or replenish our parched spirit. Sometimes we even refer to our dry times as our personal "wilderness," those barren seasons when loss or illness or estrangement of some kind urges us to *stop*. When difficulties confront us, it is not unusual for feelings of vulnerability to overwhelm any hint of future potential. We can feel stuck and empty and profoundly alone. Enveloped by such emptiness, then, we arrive at a threshold.

During such times we can feel almost paralyzed. Often we are inclined to want to "just stay put." It is here that we can tap the wisdom of the second phase of the Vision Quest, which urges the seeker to move across the threshold and into the clearing he or she has made to sit and wait. The space Native Americans clear around them is intended to echo the space they have cleared within themselves, a reflection of the inner and outer harmony central to their spiritual beliefs. It is in the deep silence and darkness that Native Americans literally "cry out" for the new vision. They trust it will come.

When we women step out of routine to sit and wait in our own lives, our initial reaction is frequently one of impatience, even agitation. Most of us aren't very good at waiting. Accustomed as we are to our busy, tightly-scheduled lives, moving into empty space can at first seem risky and unsettling, even frightening. We fear what we might uncover in the silence, or worse, that we will uncover nothing at all. Sherry Ruth Anderson and Patricia Hopkins in their book, *The Feminine Face of God*, describe the reactions this way: "When we are on the verge of making a deep promise, it is not uncommon for great resistances and fears to arise. Whatever threatens our reality or present way of life, whatever we know will profoundly change us, often seems more terrifying than inviting."

These words connect Barbara to the vivid memory of the birth of her first child:

As eager as I was to have a baby, at the onset of labor I was inexplicably plagued by questions and serious doubt. Did I have the strength to endure what lay ahead? Would my child be safely delivered? And once my child was born, would I have what it takes to parent him or her into adulthood?

These questions completely undermined my confidence. Obviously, there was no turning back, a fact that only added to my feelings of utter vulnerability and defenselessness. Little did I know then that similar doubts and fears would surface at other significant turning points in the years that followed: returning to school, changing careers, launching teenagers, losing a parent, beginning a center of feminine spirituality, writing a book. Each transition was undertaken with fear and trembling.

Yet I discovered that only when we can open ourselves fully and vulnerably are we able to make that dangerous journey from our head to our heart. It is when we move into our heart that we can begin to release our thoughts of the past and our worries about the future. Here, deep in our heart, is where we touch our passions and learn to dwell mindfully with mystery; it is in the heart that we begin to trust that we are not making this perilous journey alone.

For Native Americans, their trust is grounded in a strong belief that the earth on which they sit is sacred. As a culture they are intimately bound to the natural world and honor every aspect of creation. The earth, Mother Earth, is their Great Teacher. They know, without doubt, that they can rely on her presence and wisdom during their times of personal change and transition.

What might life have been like for the rest of us if from a young age we had been encouraged to trust our earthiness and see our own cycles of filling and emptying as wisdom? How different it would be for us to dwell in emptiness now and welcome it not as a threat but as a rich opportunity to make contact with the deepest part of ourselves, our divine center. Tapping this sacred place, we can come home to ourselves and feel the assurance that no matter what is happening in our lives, we are not facing it alone. Lingering in this cleared space may unleash our creativity and free up our imagination to reveal to us the sacred vision, fresh start, or new beginning that is buried deep in the core of who we are.

The wisdom of the final phase of the Vision Quest moves us to action and challenges us to embody the new vision we have just recently uncovered in the stillness. In Native American cultures, those who complete a Vision Quest emerge not only changed themselves but also committed to live out their new vision within their community, their tribe, despite how difficult it often is to return to our old environment and choose to live life differently.

At first, when we sense we have been changed from the inside-out (regardless of how great or small a change that might be), returning to the old order might leave us feeling uneasy, something like a misfit. It is as if we have a foot in two worlds simultaneously. In some ways, that is exactly what we are called to do. The challenge of living a new vision may be learning to live with balance and congruence in *both* of our worlds, the inner and the outer. What we touched in the stillness — our sacred center — can no longer be ignored. Its influence is ongoing and continually invites us to stay connected to the divine dream to live our lives more fully and authentically, to "walk our talk." How that happens, of course, is ultimately up to us.

A ritual like the Vision Quest won't necessarily remove the anxiety that often accompanies a time of significant change in our lives. Change will always be difficult because it dashes our sense of security and upsets the status quo. But a process like this can help connect us to our own inner wisdom and remind us that most change follows a predictable dynamic: an ending followed by a period of unsettling emptiness, which only *eventually* opens up to a fresh new beginning.

As we pay attention to this familiar cycle within and around us, we may begin to understand, as many tribal cultures do, that change is not some aberrant moment in time, something to be resisted or simply endured. The three-part cycle of the Vision Quest is truly the very pattern that undergirds and informs all of life. It is the way of growth and renewal. It is inside as well as all around us in the waxing and waning, the dyings and risings, the ebb and the flow of the natural world. It is at the very heart of our Christian tradition in what we call the Paschal Mystery — life, death, and life again.

As we prepare to engage a world, a church, and our personal lives where the winds of change are already howling, we will undoubtedly be faced with many crossroad-and-threshold moments. Some of the images here can be your invitation to pause and trust that process will unfold in its own time. As you sit and wait, may these prophetic words of Mahatma Gandhi accompany you as your companion and guide: "You must *be* the change you wish to see."

Honoring Your Experience

⊞ Name a moment in your own life that you recognized as a crossroad or threshold, even as it was occurring. What were your feelings at the time? What are your feelings now as you look back on the experience?

⊞ What are some of the things that are ending for you right now? What is starting? Which ones have the potential for truly changing your life for better or for worse?

⊞ Which of the three phases of the Native American Vision Quest — letting go, waiting for a new vision, or carrying that vision out — seems most difficult to you? Why?

Reflecting Through Ritual

Think of a dream or aspiration you hold right now in your life. Write down that vision and place it among your objects from nature. Now pray the prayer below by Teilhard de Chardin.

Moving Back into Daily Life

A prayer from *The Making of a Mind: Letters from a Soldier Priest* by Pierre Teilhard de Chardin, SJ

> Above all, trust in the slow work of God.
> We are, quite naturally,
> impatient in everything
> to reach the end without delay.
> We should like to skip
> the intermediate stages.
> We are impatient of being on the way
> to something unknown,
> something new.
>
> And yet it is the law of all progress
> that it is made by passing through some
> stages of instability.
> And that it may take a very long time.

And so I think it is with you.
Your ideas mature gradually.
Let them grow.
Let them shape themselves,
without undue haste.
Don't try to force
them on
As though you could be today
what time will make you tomorrow.

Only God could say
what this new spirit gradually
forming within you
will be.
Give the Lord the benefit of believing
that God's hand will lead you.
And accept the anxiety
of feeling yourself
in suspense
and incomplete.

"O Great Spirit," a native American chant by Adele Getty, recorded by Robert Gass (*Winds of Song* album)

O Great Spirit
Earth, Sun, Sky and Sea
You are inside
And all around me.
(Repeat seven times)

Alternate Ways of Using the Theme with Groups

If you choose to gather in a small group of friends or a large circle, we offer the following suggestions to be adapted to your group's needs and gathering space.

Creating Sacred Space for Your Circle

Dim the lights and set chairs around a table with a lighted candle set on it, as well as a dish containing pebbles or small stones along with some blank pieces of paper.

Moving Through the Process

When people arrive and enter the circle, hand each a small stone to hold. Invite each woman to place her stone to form a circle in the center of the entire group, naming one hope, dream or goal she has for the future. Then read the *Slowing Down* reflection and listen to (or sing or read together) the *Going Deeper* song, "Gather the Dreamers." As the group listens to the opening reading and song, have each woman consider the visions that she has for herself and her loved ones.

Summarize the *Reflecting on the Theme* or offer people a few moments to look back over the material quietly. Allow time for personal journaling and reflection before beginning a group conversation. You may use the *Honoring Your Experience* questions to launch the conversation and invite each participant to describe her own journey. Or you can begin by simply asking people to share something about the reflection or theme that spoke to them.

A Ritual to Connect You to Daily Life

At the conclusion of the conversation, ask the members of the group to think of a vision or dream they each hold for their own lives. Pass out paper and invite each woman to write down her vision and leave it inside the circle of stones. Then have someone read the prayer from *Moving Back into Daily Life*. Conclude by inviting the group to sing the closing chant, "O Great Spirit," together as they leave the sacred circle.

So, when we have made every effort to understand, we are ready to take upon ourselves the mystery of things; then the most trivial of happenings is touched by wonder, and there may come to us, by grace, a moment of unclouded vision.

– from *Old Age* by Helen Luke

Creating Sacred Space

Keep it simple! Place a lighted candle and an image (e.g., a photograph, a book, a symbol) that will remind you of some aspect of aging on a table next to you.

Slowing Down

A poem by Wilma Spellman (*unpublished*)

When I'm ninety or so
perhaps I'll go to India
for wisdom.
Perhaps I'll dance the tarantella
south of Rome.
Or enter a hog-calling contest right
down in Hillsborough, N.C.
I may take a train to Seattle
and live in the rain.
There's a chance I'll feed squirrels
in Grant Park
and sandwiches to
beggars like myself.

When I'm ninety or so
I'll love my silvered hair and
creaky limbs,
and oil my old machine
and laugh and sigh a lot
at life and death.
But I promise now to cry and cry
should I not dream,
should rusty grow my dreams.

Going Deeper

"Myself Growing Older," a song by Marsie Silvestro (*In Avalon* ablum)

Here I am, becoming clear
Standing strong, from my years.
I am woman growing older
Finding life in myself
Finding truth in myself
Being free.

See the lines round my eyes
Stories lived, tears I've cried
I am woman, growing older
Finding beauty in myself
Finding strength in myself
Being strong.

I have loved, hurt, and healed
Found my dreams keep me real
I am woman growing older
Finding peace in myself
Finding love in myself.
Growing old
I am clear, I am free.
I am growing strong
Here I am…I am here.

Reflecting on the Theme

Take a few minutes to reflect on your true attitudes about aging — both positive and negative. Do they include the attitude of Helen Luke in the quote that opens this chapter?

More and more women today are reminding us that the "graying of America" is hardly a pejorative term. These are women who know the value of being a "seasoned woman," and they are quick to point out that what they represent is a down-to-earth wisdom that does not come automatically just because a woman reaches a ripened age. The wisdom they exude is the outcome of an intentional process that began years earlier in the choices and decisions they made along the way. Clearly, theirs is a wisdom that is laced with hard work and grace.

Many of us in our sixties, regardless of how vital and productive we seem to be, are concerned not only about our own aging process but also about the inevitability of an enforced rite of passage that will determine the end of our careers and some of our life choices as well.

Despite scientific evidence that suggests we can live fit and healthy well into our eighties and beyond, most of us are fully aware that our Western culture does not look sympathetically on the aging process and chooses to see the arbitrary age of the mid-sixties as the end of productive living. This bias is supported in all areas of the media, who reinforce through image and inference the cultural myth that youthful zest and beauty are still the cherished ideal. Isn't it true that we are quick to celebrate whatever is fresh and new? As a result, we are left with a poverty of images and role models for what it means to age with grace.

Men are certainly subject to the effects of these negative images and mindsets. Still, on a purely physical level, we often hear an aging male described as "distinguished," "mature," or even "wise." Compare that to the descriptors ordinarily assigned to a woman over sixty-five: "past her prime," "dowdy," "matronly," or "hag." Because language has the power to influence both behavior and self-image, it becomes clear that for an aging woman it would take significant effort and determination to overcome such a debilitating cultural bias. This becomes more problematic still when we take into consideration women's longer life expectancy and the recent statistics that suggest a female child born in the year 2003 has the potential to live to be one hundred years old — thirty-five years beyond what our society now considers old age.

It is hardly the intention of the two of us to dilute or deny the unavoidable challenges and losses associated with the aging process. However, it is our intention to illustrate how the prevailing attitudes and stereotypes not only discriminate against women in particular but also severely distort our sense of our deepest selves and the possibilities still open to women in their fifties, sixties, seventies, eighties and beyond.

In truth, we are all aging. Hour by hour and day by day every part of us is undergoing subtle shifts and changes. While most of us will not recognize this phenomenon until the changes become obvious or visible, we are all engaged in an ongoing process of some degree of diminishment. We can, bowing to pressure from our culture, attempt to resist and disguise these changes. Or we can begin to pay attention to them and become aware of the invitation buried inside both our body's and our soul's natural responses to their changing patterns and energies.

To do this we might turn once again to the wisdom of feminine spirituality. A feminine spirituality attempts to uproot *either/or* thinking and open us instead to a broader perspective that, in this case, allows us to see aging not only as a time of liability and limitation but as a time of unlimited possibility as well.

Several women who have weathered many seasons and cycles of life come to us regularly for spiritual direction to reflect upon the reality of their later years. One in particular, a woman in her mid-eighties, speaks frankly of her physical challenges with advancing arthritis. She describes with candor her occasional bouts of loneliness as a widow, the sole survivor in her family of origin, and the mother of eight adults, all now engaged in pursuits of their own. This phase of her life is drastically different from those that preceded it, but she is quick to point out that such difference is not all bad news. Many of the activities and engagements that occupied her in earlier years are no longer a concern for her. In their place, she has found time for solitude and reflection as well as a new willingness to open herself to a deeper relationship with her God.

This woman describes an "inner spaciousness" that seems to bring her into contact with her own deep wisdom, something she savors and nurtures with art and poetry, music and beauty — things she had considered sheer luxury while juggling a household of ten. Though she is certainly no stranger to thoughts of death, she mentions that much of what she suffers these days are like a series of "little deaths" along the way. She believes these are ongoing invitations to help her begin to let go and to make room for new ideas and insights trying to emerge. Grappling with these "little deaths," she says, also helps her to prepare for what inevitably lies ahead.

A reflective woman such as this one offers the rest of us a clearer understanding of the great paradox of the aging process: There is physical decline, to be sure; yet such diminishment can sometimes signal an experience of rich inner growth. Contemplation, reflection and solitude at this age seem to allow us both to look back *and* to look ahead.

A woman later in life can reflect on her entire life story and — like a quilter — may come to terms at last with some of life's painful pieces, while noticing, perhaps for the first time, the sacred moments that were interspersed throughout. Such sifting and sorting can help her grasp the meaning of her life and may set the course for imagining what legacies and graces she will be leaving to the next generation.

Whether she chooses it for herself or has it foisted upon her by her waning energies, a woman's cultivation of stillness and time for personal reflection seem to be hallmarks of healthy aging. Indeed, they are signs of spiritual growth at whatever stage of the life cycle we happen to be. Slowing down allows us to tap into our inner resources and awaken to our deep potential. It is often at such moments that some of us begin to sense our intimate connection to the sacred.

In her poignant book, *Winter Grace*, Kathleen Fischer reminds us how we tend to perceive a woman's life as following the pattern of the seasons, with old age corresponding to the winter time of life: stark and barren. If we view aging from a strictly cultural or biological perspective — highlighting our aches and pains, our losses and limitations — then perhaps this description fits. However, Fischer calls our attention to a line in Annie Dillard's book, *Pilgrim at Tinker Creek*, that seems to contradict that view and offers a more hopeful and creative alternative: "I bloom indoors in the winter like a forced forsythia; I must come in to come out."

"I must come in." It's time to cultivate my inner life; to make peace with broken promises and broken dreams; to forgive myself and others for what might never be; to begin to touch the mystery inherent in both our joys *and* our sufferings. When we "come in" to do such deep inner work, our "coming out" will undoubtedly result in a blossoming that is both enduring and real.

Such blossoming is modeled by the zesty octogenarian who shows us what it means to move into our later years with age, grace and wisdom. While rare in our contemporary culture, she is not alone. She is among a new genre of aging women who are pioneering different and even revolutionary attitudes by refusing to allow our society to determine how they will live out their lives. Indeed, perspectives on aging are undergoing a revolution, much of it because of a handful of feisty elder women who are reclaiming their power to define their own unique reality.

If we look closely we will notice evidence of this shift of consciousness all around us in circles of women who are gathering in widely disparate settings. For example, "croning ceremonies," rituals that honor women ages fifty-six through seventy and beyond for their wisdom born over a lifetime of both challenging and exhilarating experiences, are proliferating in our country and around the world. Historically, a crone was a spiritual elder and wisdom figure to whom others looked for insight and support in moments of transition and change.

Chapters of the National Red Hat Society are emerging all across the country where members sporting purple garb and red hats gather to celebrate their common-sense wisdom and their defiant hope in the face of having survived a series of life's hardships and triumphs.

Book and study groups on topics of aging are surfacing in record numbers in women's groups, churches, health clubs and senior centers around the country. (Kathleen Fischer, Maria Harris, Betty Freidan, Ruth Jacobs, May Sarton, Helen Luke, and Simone de Beauvoir are just some of the authors who provide rich material for discussion and practice.)

The women in these and other circles are the mentors and models for the next generation. They witness to all of us how healthy aging is not a cosmetic concern, nor is it simply a matter of determination or an act of the will. It comes from a deeper place, an inner freedom — grace that becomes so obvious that by her sheer presence a woman can powerfully contradict the prevailing stereotype of the older woman as useless and used up.

Honoring Your Experience

▦ What are some of the qualities and values you wish to see mature and ripen in you as you age? What are the choices you could make now to help this become a reality?

▦ Take time to call to mind a woman you consider a wise elder. What about this person attracts you? Do you see any of her qualities in yourself?

▦ Name three significant things about being the age you are right now.

Reflecting Through Ritual

Find a mirror and hold it up to your face. Examine the lifelines age has given you — wrinkles, age spots, gray hair, etc. Take a moment to authentically admire the beauty that dwells there on your face. As you go about your day, wear those marks of time like badges of honor — commemorating the wisdom, beauty, courage and strength within that has come not simply in spite of age but because of it.

Moving Back into Daily Life

A reading from *Women Who Run with the Wolves* by Clarissa Pinkola Estés

> It is a good idea for women to count their ages, not by years, but by battle scars. "How old are you?" people sometimes ask me. "I'm seventeen battle scars old," I say. Usually people don't flinch, and rather happily begin to count up their own battle scars accordingly…. I wonder what our granddaughters and great-granddaughters will think of our lives recorded accordingly. I hope it will all have to be explained to them…for you have earned it by the hard choices of your life.

A poem by Donna M. Williams, SLW *(unpublished)*

> Aging is deepened
> Creativity.
> Transformation happening.
>
> Aging is wisdom
> Revisiting and
> Reclaiming one's life.

"How Could Anyone," a song by Libby Roderick (*If You See a Dream* album)

> How could anyone ever tell you
> You are anything less than beautiful
> How could anyone ever tell you
>
> You are less than whole?
> How could anyone fail to notice
> That your loving is a miracle
> How deeply you're connected to my soul?

Alternate Ways of Using the Theme with Groups

If you choose to gather in a small group of friends or a large circle, we offer the following suggestions to be adapted to your group's needs and gathering space.

Creating Sacred Space for Your Circle

Place a circle of chairs around a low table covered with purple cloth and a lighted candle placed on top of it, alongside a jaunty red hat. Scatter a variety of books on the topic of women and aging around you.

Moving Through the Process

Invite participants to join the circle and introduce themselves by telling how they feel about the process of aging…and why. Then read the *Slowing Down* reflection and listen to (or sing or read together) the *Going Deeper* song, "Myself Growing Older." As the group listens to the opening reading and song, have each woman think about the aging process.

Summarize the *Reflecting on the Theme* or offer people a few moments to look back over the material quietly. Allow time for personal journaling and reflection before beginning a group conversation. You may use the *Honoring Your Experience* questions to launch the conversation and invite each participant to describe her own journey. Or you can begin by simply asking people to share something about the reflection or theme that spoke to them.

A Ritual to Connect You to Daily Life

Invite each woman to stand and join hands with the person on either side of her. Have someone read one or both of the two readings from *Moving Back into Daily Life*. Lead the group through a guided meditation of themselves at age ten, twenty, thirty, forty, fifty, sixty, seventy, eighty, ninety. Conclude by singing (or reading together) the mantra "How Could Anyone."

STREAMS OF WELLNESS

Let the beauty you love be what you do.
There are a hundred ways to kneel and kiss the ground.

– Jelaluddin Rumi, thirteenth-century Sufi poet

Creating Sacred Space

Keep it simple! Ancient cultures believed stones had the power to activate sacred healing energy. Place a few stones on a table near a candle to symbolize your desire to be healed and to be whole.

Slowing Down

A poem by Jan L. Richardson from *Night Visions*

For all that enfolds us
    for each word of grace
    and every act of care;

for those who offer refuge
    for each shelter given
    and for every welcoming space;

for the healing of our souls
    for balm and rest
    for soothing and sleep;

for vigils kept
    and for lights kept burning;

blessed be!

Going Deeper

"Song of Sorrow and Healing," a song by Carolyn McDade (*Sorrow and Healing* album)

> Be there Spirit of the Wind
> Breathe in me
> Spirit of the Sun,
> Rekindle my flame
> Spirit of the Rain,
> Fill my dry and deep recesses
> Spirit of the Land,
> Raise me again.
>
> Deep in your cry lifts the wind.
> Deep in your tear falls the healing rain.
> Deep in your love shines radiant sun.
> Deep in your life your land lives on!

Reflecting on the Theme

Take a few minutes now to think about the various kinds of "dis-ease" — physical, psychological, spiritual — you have experienced in your life. Now remember the various kinds of medicine that healed you.

There is a remarkable revolution taking place in the field of medicine as women begin birthing new attitudes and fresh ways of looking at health and healing. Gone are the days when we as women sat by passively as someone else — frequently a complete stranger — mapped out a course of treatment for us. Gone, too, is the belief that medicine is only something we pick up at the local pharmacy and ingest. Statistics indicate that we are increasingly redefining what health and healing mean for us. Today we are more informed and involved, searching out an array of practices and techniques that not only help relieve symptoms but also contribute to a more holistic experience of wellness and well-being. Indeed, as women we are beginning to take charge of our own health.

Some women exhibit amazing creativity and imagination as they seek their own path to healing. Jane, for example, suffered for many years with rheumatoid arthritis, a condition that causes severe joint pain that progressively limited her mobility and created a great deal of stress and anxiety for her and her family. She underwent a battery of medical tests and techniques in search of healing. At a particularly low point, Jane enrolled in a meditation class. After just ten sessions, she began to notice some relief of her symptoms and a positive change in her attitude.

Then there was Clare, who had a sudden recurrence of breast cancer, even though she had carefully followed the healing regimen prescribed by her physician for an entire year. She felt distraught by the return of her disease. Clare was also terrified by what she believed was the grim inevitability of the disease's progression. "But I am not one to give up," she proclaimed. Consequently, she agreed to undergo another round of chemotherapy to fight the cancer, knowing that this time she needed something to soothe her soul as well. She joined a group practicing the ancient Asian exercise *Qi Gong* amid the colorful beauty of a local botanical garden.

Recently both Jane and Clare arrived in the same circle to reflect on their unique stories of healing. Many of us sitting in that circle had already begun to recognize how conventional medicine is just one way of treating illness. Most of us had also heard reports of some amazing biological recoveries that could not be explained in scientific terms. Yet as these women began to tell their stories, something powerful happened. No longer were these mere statistics but real women — tears running down their cheeks, speaking from their own experiences of pain. They could be our sisters, friends, co-workers; they could be any of us! Their stories were both personal and compelling. What they shared that day demonstrated convincingly that medicine, as we have long defined it, is changing. More and more of us are becoming involved in our own healing. Certainly there are many women like Clare and Jane who are at the forefront of this change.

As women, we often have a tangible connection to our bodies. Our monthly menses, as well as pregnancy, childbirth and menopause all link us into our body's gentle rhythms, whispering to us of its sacred powers. Because many of us access wisdom through our body, it is important for us to pay close attention to its shifts and changes, to listen to its signs and symptoms. Because we know our own body best, women are stepping up to challenge the dualisms so prevalent in traditional health care systems that insist on separating body from spirit and even life from death. Many of us have long intuited that healing is not confined to care of the body through conventional medicine alone. We know healing is holistic and involves care of our body, mind *and* soul. In *A Woman's Journey to God*, Joan Borysenko supports this belief. "The word *healing* comes from the old Anglo-Saxon word *haelan*, which means 'wholeness' — body, mind, and spirit," she explains. "Spirituality and healing, really, are one and the same thing."

Indeed, what women are discovering today is truly revolutionary. We know that medicine and other tools for healing can take many different forms: images and symbols, poetry and art, music and prayer, meditation and energy work, yoga and beauty, laughter and deep friendship, even our very breath. We "gather medicine" not only to treat our physical ailments but to keep our souls alive as well. While there are certainly many who are wary of this idea, more and more women are reclaiming the power to name what is healing for us. We are beginning to demand that our specific needs be taken seriously.

In this revolution we are being mentored by medical professionals such as Joan Borysenko, Christiane Northrup, Rachel Naomi Remen, Mona Lisa Schulz and Elisabeth Kubler-Ross, to name just a few. These are women scientists who have spent years researching the body-mind-spirit connection. They were among the first to acknowledge how the boundaries between medicine and spirituality have become blurred. Additionally, they remind us that women have a long history of being healers, though over time we have certainly paid dearly for this power: We have been ignored and dismissed because of it, and in the Middle Ages women were actually imprisoned and persecuted for it. During the Colonial period in Salem, Massachusetts, our wisdom was labeled "witchcraft" and we were burned on stakes for sharing it. Today, women are no longer willing to be forced underground. Scores of us have moved from feeling like a victim to feeling empowered. This fact becomes apparent every time we sit in circles of caring and listen to one another's stories. We hear again and again that many, like Jane and Clare, are finally ready to rise up and reclaim the power of our ancestors to heal and be healed in our own ways.

What we are learning is that while each of us may hold different images and views of God, sacred healing energy is common to us all. Indeed, it is something that is within as well as around each one of us. Yet there are many different paths and as many different ways to evoke it. Our challenge is to learn how to access this sacred energy for ourselves.

Let's return to Clare. As she began to search out the various pathways to her "Inner Healer," she turned first to the wisdom of her own Christian tradition, weaving in other religions and cultures as well. In the process, she stumbled upon the Medicine Wheel, a centerpiece of Native American spirituality. Often called a *circle of life*, the Medicine Wheel expands our understanding of the healing properties inherent in the natural world.

Clare was drawn to this image not only because nature has always been a source of comfort and solace for her but also because the image itself — a circle of stones honoring each of the four directions — spoke to her belief that the truth comes from many directions, just as healing comes through many different sources. She knew from her extensive reading how exposure to nature helps promote good health and speeds up the healing process. In fact, she spoke with great animation as she recalled how her favorite childhood heroine, Florence Nightingale, the founder of modern nursing, often placed bouquets of freshly-picked flowers in patients' rooms because she noticed that doing so actually helped hasten their recovery.

The link between natural beauty and healing was familiar to Clare. Inspired by what she was uncovering, she crafted a medicine wheel of her own that now sits on her coffee table. She placed a small circle of stones gathered from around her home, and carefully marked off the four directions with larger ones. Every morning Clare repeats a simple ritual of turning to the North, South, East and West, seeking from each the wisdom and courage she needs to walk with health and beauty into her day. This ritual has become especially important to her as she undergoes rigorous treatments to halt the spread of her disease. Alone, this practice may not cure her cancer, but she notices these days how both her anger and anxiety have been significantly reduced — evidence of some deep and necessary healing.

Each of us has our own particular way of "gathering medicine" to help us stay in the struggle of life and do the hard work of change. Perhaps yours is a long morning walk or time spent doing needlework or gardening, sharing in a support group, or talking with a friend over a cup of tea. It might mean learning how to deal with anger, walk away from a toxic relationship, or speak out against some personal or social injustice. The particulars are not nearly as important as our intentional commitment to some spiritual practice. Generations of healers and shamans tell us that "where intention goes, energy flows."

As we name for ourselves the ways in which we try to access this healing energy, we might begin to notice within us and around us many streams of wellness and many ways to gather medicine. What is common to each is the invitation to find our balance, seek direction for our lives, and trust that each of us carries a piece of healing truth.

These are examples of how ordinary women are taking back the power over their bodies. We women know healing is so much more than a sheer act of the will or the result of high technology. It is more than mere technique. "Each of us has a technique, perhaps several…that is a vehicle for healing," affirms Rachel Naomi Remen, M.D. "We have to ask, beyond these techniques, what it is that truly fosters the healing process."

Ultimately, each of us must answer that question for ourselves, but the wisdom we continue to uncover as we gather our own medicine seems to challenge us to remain open and receptive to the Great Mystery at the core of who we are. Perhaps it is only as we connect to this Mystery — our own Inner Healer — and remain true to ourselves that the real meaning of healing will be revealed. Only then will medicine and spirituality finally have come together for us.

Honoring Your Experience

▨ What is "wellness" for you? Write a definition from your own experience.

▨ Is there a particular way or technique you use to access your Inner Healer? Describe it in detail.

▨ Describe a time when you were "healed" by something other than traditional Western medicine.

Reflecting Through Ritual

Take the stones you placed next to you and make a pilgrimage with them around your home. Place one in your medicine cabinet to remind you that healing does not only come out of a medicine bottle but also from the sacred within. Place another in your refrigerator to remind you to eat healthy food. Place others in places you will come across them on a regular basis to remind you that sacred healing energy is available all around you.

Moving Back into Daily Life

A reading from "A Spiritual Director Reflects on Illness, Healing and Death" by Rita L. Petrusa, OP, in *Journey's Companion*, a publication of the Institute for Spiritual Leadership

> Healing is different from curing. I have come to know that there are many levels on which healing can happen — emotional, spiritual, mental, and probably others…. Healing means…being able to hold all possible outcomes, living with the unknown, and trusting in Ultimate Goodness — that even if my body dies, the essence of who I am is safe and will never die. I truly believe this.

"Go in Beauty," a song by William Ryder (*Songs of Healing* album)

> Go in beauty
> Peace be with you,
> Till we meet again
> In the light.
> (repeat seven times)

Alternate Ways of Using the Theme with Groups

If you choose to gather in a small group of friends or a large circle, we offer the following suggestions to be adapted to your group's needs and gathering space.

Creating Sacred Space for Your Circle

Place a solitary lighted candle on the center of the floor. Place four stones, pointing North, South, East, and West around it, forming a simple Medicine Wheel.

Moving Through the Process

As participants enter the space, hand each woman a stone to hold. Invite each woman to introduce herself by naming one way she has already been healed and then placing her stone in a circle around the candle. Then read the *Slowing Down* reflection and listen to (or sing or read together) the *Going Deeper* song, "Song of Sorrow and Healing." As the group listens to the opening reading and song, have each woman focus on what she needs healed in her life right now.

Summarize the *Reflecting on the Theme* or offer people a few moments to look back over the material quietly. Allow time for personal journaling and reflection before beginning a group conversation. You may use the *Honoring Your Experience* questions to launch the conversation and invite each participant to describe her own journey. Or you can begin by simply asking people to share something about the reflection or theme that spoke to them.

A Ritual to Connect You to Daily Life

Have the entire group stand together at the point of the Medicine Wheel facing North and pray silently for healing. Then have the group repeat this ritual facing South, East and West. Have someone read the reading from *Moving Back into Daily Life.* Conclude by singing (or reading together) the song "Go in Beauty."

Part IV

SURRENDERING TO THE SEASONS

Gleaning the Wisdom

SUMMER: UNBURYING WONDER

I was by God's side, a master craftswoman,
delighting God day after day, ever at play in God's presence,
at play everywhere in the world,
delighting to be with the children of the earth.

– adapted from Proverbs 8:30-31

Creating Sacred Space

Keep it simple! Place a lighted candle on a table next to you, along with symbols of summer, such as a photograph from a favorite summer vacation, a beach towel, or sandals.

Slowing Down
"The Summer Day," a poem from *New and Selected Poems by Mary Oliver*

Who made the world?
Who made the swan, and the black bear?
Who made the grasshopper?
This grasshopper, I mean —
the one who has flung herself out of the grass,
the one who is eating sugar out of my hand,
who is moving her jaws back and forth instead of up and down —
who is gazing around with her enormous and complicated eyes.
Now she lifts her pale forearms and thoroughly washes her face.
Now she snaps her wings open, and floats away.
I don't know exactly what a prayer is.
I do know how to pay attention, how to fall down
into the grass, how to kneel down in the grass,
how to be idle and blessed, how to stroll through the fields,
which is what I have been doing all day.
Tell me, what else should I have done?
Doesn't everything die at last, and too soon?
Tell me, what is it you plan to do
with your one wild and precious life?

Going Deeper

"Spirit of Life," a song by Carolyn McDade (*We Come with Our Voices* album)

> Spirit of Life, come unto me
> Sing in my heart all the stirrings of compassion.
> Blow in the wind, rise in the sea
> Move in the hand giving life the shape of justice.
> Roots hold me close, wings set me free.
> Spirit of Life, come to me
> Come to me.

Reflecting on the Theme

Take a few minutes to be with your own recollections of summertime. If it feels appropriate, kick off your shoes and imagine yourself walking barefoot in the sand or on freshly-mown grass.

Summer is the season of abundance and rejuvenation, a time when Mother Earth opens wide her warm embrace. For those of us living in the northern hemisphere, summer's arrival has a particular appeal; it comes not only as a welcome relief from the rigors of harsh and unforgiving winters but also as a wondrous gift that reminds us once again that death does not have the final word and that nothing is impossible with our Creator God.

With flowers and trees bursting into blossom all around us, this season seems to entice every woman to unbind herself of the many layers that have confined her over the winter months and allow the earth to heal and restore her. Some of us may even feel the urge to walk barefoot on the sacred earth now in full bloom. Moving unencumbered in this way can help us get in touch with the innocence and simplicity of earlier summers, those times when bathing suits and bare feet were the dress of the day, when building a sandcastle was a passport to an exotic world, and when laughter and play were the only business at hand. This was a time long before we felt the need to be programmed and productive, when we were free "just to be" and to revel in the gifts of creation.

Such freedom is the summer's spiritual invitation to each of us. As temperatures rise and the pace of life slows down, we are drawn each summer to become like little children once again, to lighten our hearts and to let life flow through us as we immerse ourselves in earth's beauty.

Responding to such an invitation may come naturally to some; but for those of us who are governed by a strong work ethic, slowing down can be difficult. Most of us are culturally programmed to make the best use of our talents through busy schedules and productive lives. Even our leisure time can seem like pretty serious business. However, summer's brilliant arrival somehow awakens even the most industrious among us to the reality that making room for the carefree energy of our youth may be exactly what we need to help restore balance to our lives and begin to recover a sense of joy.

So where do we begin? How do we go about learning to become carefree and to reclaim our capacity for joy?

When we are seeking to learn most skills, we turn to experts or wise ones around us. In this case, the "experts" are children. Taking time to observe a young child at play may reveal a whole new way of understanding what prayer is all about. The passion and enthusiasm with which children engage in their play — digging intently in the sandbox or blowing the seeds from a dandelion head or gleefully catching fireflies in a jar — is a thrill to observe. Indeed, children are models of spontaneity and delight in the way they open themselves to exploring the wonder that is all around them.

Perhaps it was this connection between child's play and prayer that inspired Mary Oliver to write the poem, "The Summer Day," reproduced in the *Slowing Down* section above. She magically captures through word and image not only the childlike abandon of her experience of nature but its transcendent quality as well.

Jesus, in his teachings, made several specific references to the significant role children play in our lives. He urged us to welcome them, make room for them, spend time with them; ultimately, he said, *a little child will lead us* (see Isaiah 11:6).

As we follow their lead, we might discover how often children remind us that it is the simple things — a wildflower, a butterfly, the splash of a wave — that can link us to mystery and help us uncover the wonder at the very core of our life. When we open ourselves to such wonder — to the awesome Presence dwelling in our very depths — something powerful gets unleashed in us, something that is difficult to contain. For some of us, such an experience may initiate an inward journey of contemplation, a time of stillness where we can dwell quietly with the enormous beauty we find within and all around us. Others may feel the call to share this wonder creatively with others, for sharing wonder is one of the ways each of us is invited into the sacred act of co-creation.

Again, some of us may shy away from such an invitation because — unlike the child — we are hard on ourselves. Often we are our own worst critics and tend to reject our capacity to be creative. Perhaps this is the outcome of being raised with a narrow definition of creativity, thinking of the act of creation only in terms of making the "professional" art found in fancy museums or lofty performance halls. We may carry the false belief that if we are not an acclaimed artist we are simply not creative.

However, the creative spirit is a vital part of each one of us. "Creativity is God's gift to us," Julia Cameron says in her empowering book *The Artist's Way*. "Using our creativity is our gift back to God." Our creativity, then, is not only our birthright; it becomes our responsibility as well. It might help us claim our creativity if we begin to consider that *any* imaginative act — anything into which we pour out our soul in order to enhance life — is our gift back to our Creator God.

Consider, for a moment, some of the ways we women enhance life by creating beauty in our homes, gardens, workplaces, and in the lives of those whom we love. One woman we both know prepares a lovely dinner and serves it *al fresco* for all her neighbors every year on the evening of summer's first full moon; another brings to her office each week unique arrangements of freshly-cut zinnias from her garden; a young mother packs up the beach cooler — rain or shine — for an impromptu indoor/outdoor picnic each week with her toddlers; still another calls together her closest women friends for an annual summer solstice gathering. Probably none of these women would call themselves an artist, yet each demonstrates a particular ability to enliven the spirits of those around them by creating experiences and environments of beauty and joy. Each has the gift of co-creating in her own way, making visible the invisible to those around her.

Their stories and others might suggest that creativity is simply a matter of falling in love with life. When we think of creativity in these terms, then just about anything we do with love can become a creative act. Like a child, we too might begin to experience life as art, where our lives themselves can become our masterpiece — our unique contribution to the Holy One and to the world around us as well.

Certainly creativity can shift our perspective. So much of what we call "creative thinking" is really the result of looking with fresh eyes at ordinary experiences and finding in them the extraordinary. It is what we often refer to as *unburying the wonder in our midst* or *finding the sacred in the everyday*.

Perhaps that was the experience of the poet Elizabeth Barrett Browning when she wrote:

> Earth's crammed with heaven,
> And every common bush afire with God;
> But only he who sees, takes off his shoes —
> The rest sit 'round it and pluck blackberries....

Such is the wonder that surrounds us each summer, luring us to pause, to play, and to reclaim the vision of the small child. Only when we live as children do — with our eyes wide open, breathing in the colors of the sea, the grass, the blossoms and the sky — can we proclaim with awe the poetic words of Gerard Manley Hopkins: "The world is charged with the glory of God!" Can we give ourselves over to such wonder? Can we allow our hearts to open so fully, to let our imaginations run wild? Can we be free enough to take off our shoes and trust that the earth on which we stand is truly holy ground?

Lingering with questions such as these in the midst of summer's intoxicating beauty may offer us a glimpse at the meaning of wisdom and a hint at how we might begin to imagine *our* part in renewing the face of the earth.

Honoring Your Experience

- Make a list of some ways you are creative. Don't be afraid to add mundane things that are never considered "art," such as picking out clothes for yourself or others, making up impromptu prayers, or organizing birthday parties.

- Think of three ways you might deepen the connection in your spiritual life between your prayer and your play.

- Describe a child you know who just tickles you to death!

Reflecting Through Ritual

If the weather permits, wander outside, walk barefoot on the ground, and allow the sights, smells and textures of the season to awaken your senses. Take some time to journal or sketch your responses to this experience. (If the weather is bad, take a walk in the rain or snow. If that is impossible, then take a "virtual" walk in your imagination through a place you love.)

Moving Back into Daily Life

A reading from *Seasons of Your Heart* by Macrina Wiederkehr

Taking off your shoes is a sacred ritual. It is a hallowed moment of remembering the goodness of space and time. It is a way of celebrating the *holy ground* on which you stand. If you want to be a child of wonder, cherish the truth that time and space are holy. Whether you take off your shoes symbolically or literally matters little. What is important is that you are alive to the *holy ground* on which you stand and to the *holy ground* that you are.

"Low to the Ground," a song by Libby Roderick (*Thinking Like a Mountain* album)

We stand on the edge of a cliff
In the deepest night I've ever seen
People looking for light
People who cherish a dream.
But the light's shining out from our eyes
And the dream's resting deep in our souls
It's magic we need to keep us from falling
It's magic we already know.

Chorus:
It's music that keeps us alive
It's dancing that sets our hearts free
It's children remember the laughter in life
It's animals teach us to see.
Stay low to the ground
Live close to the earth
Don't stray very far from your soul
It's simple things show us the reason we're here
And it's simple things keeping us whole.

Tell me the place you were born
The lives that your ancestors led
The ground that surrounded the people you love
The streams from which you were fed
It's the wind that carries the seed
And the seed that carries the song
The food that we're eating is rooted in soil
And it's soil that is keeping us strong.

The temples are falling around us
We stand strong and fierce where they've been
I never have seen a holier sight
Than a person who sings in the wind.
Our blood is the river of life
Our joy is the sun on the land
All of the love that is inside this heart
Is more than one person can stand.

"I Am Standing on Holy Ground," a song by Kathy Sherman, CSJ (*Coming Home* album)

I am standing on Holy Ground.
Where I'm standing is Holy Ground.
(repeat five times)

Alternate Ways of Using the Theme with Groups

If you choose to gather in a small group of friends or a large circle, we offer the following suggestions to be adapted to your group's needs and gathering space.

Creating Sacred Space for Your Circle

If you meet during the day, consider gathering outdoors. Or, if you are indoors, prepare a table with a lighted candle and symbols of summer (e.g., a beach towel, a child's sand bucket, a bottle of bubbles, a pair of sunglasses, a small bouquet of wildflowers, etc.).

Moving Through the Process

As participants enter the space, invite them to remove their shoes and build a circle with them as a symbolic gesture of openness to all that the season of summer can offer us. Invite each woman to share a favorite summer memory. Then read the *Slowing Down* reflection and listen to (or sing or read together) the *Going Deeper* song, "Spirit of Life." As the group listens to the opening reading and song, have each woman reflect on how she played as a child and how she plays now.

Summarize the *Reflecting on the Theme* or offer people a few moments to look back over the material quietly. Allow time for personal journaling and reflection before beginning a group conversation. You may use the *Honoring Your Experience* questions to launch the conversation and invite each participant to describe her own journey. Or you can begin by simply asking people to share something about the reflection or theme that spoke to them.

A Ritual to Connect You to Daily Life

If you are outside, invite the group to join hands and stroll barefoot through the yard. If you are inside, do the same through the entire space available to you. When you return to the circle, have participants put on their shoes as someone reads the reading from *Moving Back into Daily Life*. Conclude by singing (or reading together) the song "Low to the Ground" and the mantra "I Am Standing on Holy Ground."

FALL: A SOLEMN HARVEST

For everything there is a season,
and a time for every matter under heaven;
a time to be born, and a time to die;
a time to plant, and a time to pluck up
what is planted….

– Ecclesiastes 3:1-2

Creating Sacred Space

Keep it simple! On some colorful fabric draped over a table, place a floating candle in a small bowl of water, some fruit, a few leaves, and any other symbols of autumn.

Slowing Down

An excerpt from "Autumn Sonnets," by May Sarton from *At Seventy*

If I can let go as trees let go
Their leaves, so casually, one by one;
If I can come to know what they do know,
That fall is the release, the consummation,
Then fear of time and the uncertain fruit
Would not distemper the great lucid skies
This strangest autumn, mellow and acute.
If I can take the dark with open eyes
And call it seasonal, not harsh or strange
(For love itself may need a time of sleep),
And, tree like, stand unmoved before the change
Lose what I lose to keep what I can keep
The strong root still alive under the snow
Love will endure.

Going Deeper

"The Power of Letting Go," a song by Chris Spheeris, sung by Shaina Noll (*You Can Relax Now* album)

I once was a leaf among leaves on a tree
Where I grew and I shaded the things beneath me
When the wind blew strong I held the tree tight
When the sun lit the heavens I reached for the light.

And I passed many days without worry or care
'Till asleep I awakened to change in the air.
And the wind brought a chill, I grew stiff in the cold,
My color turned pale, and my hands wouldn't hold.

Now a leaf that is free, how I spiral and float
To the water below, and I ride like a boat.
And I float off to places I never would know,
Through the power of letting go.

I once was a wave, I was steady and strong.
In the rhythm of ripples, I traveled along.
And I crossed a great distance that all looked the same
A wave among waves in a place with no name.

Time went by and a shoreline appeared
Whispering of changes and endings I feared.
And I couldn't go back and I wouldn't go under,
So I road to the sand in the foam and the thunder.

Now a splash from the wave and I dance to the skies,
Where the sun makes me vapor and weightless I rise.
And I'm carried to places I never would know
Through the power of letting go.

Reflecting on the Theme

Take a few moments to reflect on the theme of fall: Get in touch with an aspect of letting go in your own life that you want to bring to prayer at this time.

During fall, as the days are getting shorter and most of us are wondering where summer went, Mother Earth is preparing to let go and move on. She seems to know better than we that the true nature of life, as Clarissa Pinkola Estés reminds us, is "to grow, to give, to get used up, and to leave seed for the new!" Perhaps it is no accident that All Soul's Day and Thanksgiving are poignantly situated in the center of this season that is not afraid of death. Now, with bowls of fruit and dead leaves, candles, and the growing awareness that the ground itself is holy, we as women are invited to celebrate a solemn harvest, holding the tension between gratitude and lamentation, learning how to let go and give thanks all at once.

As we do this, we are not alone. We stand in solidarity with our ancestors who lived in harmony with the earth and knew in their bones the importance of honoring the passing of the seasons with ritual and prayer. We connect with the mystics in every religious tradition who frequently spoke of a kinship with all of creation. And we take up the call of Jesus, who lived close to the earth and frequently drew upon its wisdom. He often used images of empty nets and full barns, the top of the mountain and the inevitable journey down as metaphors to speak of what the call to discipleship was all about.

Instead of encouraging us to resist our own mortality and inevitable losses, the fall season reminds us that our spiritual work is to honor once again the life/death/life cycle and live it with as much grace and wisdom as we know how. In contrast to the world view that sees life as moving from beginning to end, from birth to death, the autumn landscape challenges us to embrace a more cyclical understanding of the universe. It helps us see how death and letting go are part of a much larger process, one that is intimately connected to new life — if we can trust in the ebb and flow. In a similar way, it introduces us to the Paschal Mystery as it is meant to unfold in our personal lives as well.

With arms full of fruit from the harvest and fallen leaves crunching under our feet, we are reminded in simple ways that there is a rhythm to things. As we realize this, we begin to see life differently. Suddenly, change becomes the norm and stability an illusion. We become keenly aware of the recurring patterns of light and darkness, life and death, joy and heartache in our world, our churches, and our personal lives as well: Grandma dies and granddaughter is born; one generation gives way to another. The seeds of one decade become the harvest of the next. Along with the complex community of life around us, we are challenged to take in the temporary quality of life, learning the fine art of surrender as we live the cycles and seasons of our own lives as well.

Becoming more attuned to the fact that life and death are not opposites but flow into one another is not an easy task for any of us. Nor is letting go of control. However, learning how to make room for decline so that new life can emerge becomes the sacred vital work of this harvest season. As we move through our own birthings and endings, grievings and celebrations, we come to recognize a larger mystery at work, calling us to trust that life is changed, not taken away.

Elizabeth O'Connor wrote, "Each stage of life holds us upon its knees and teaches us new lessons in letting go." Perhaps it is no accident that so much of the work of the fall season brings us to our knees. Bringing a crop to harvest is hard work, almost as hard as learning how to let go and say thank you all at once. As we look back on barren fields and carry with us memories of those who have gone before us, we are confronted with the fact that letting go is no more of an option for us than it is for Mother Earth. We cannot keep a child from growing or ourselves from aging or life from changing, any more than a tree can keep its leaves intact — nor would we want to. Life is what it is; our challenge is coming to accept it on its own terms.

As Clarissa Pinkola Estés points out, the pattern is this: "In all dying, there is a uselessness that becomes useful as we pick our way through it." All of us know those times when we have dug our feet into the ground, stiffened our bodies, tightened our jaws, and demanded rational explanations for things that are unexplainable — all part of the process of picking our way through life. Yet part of us knows the futility that comes with resisting and refusing to go with the flow.

Prayer during this autumn season is mostly heart work — taking a deep breath, allowing the slow work of yielding to take place, letting the tears come to water the ground, making room for mystery, trusting our intuition, opening our hands little by little. Through it all, we are being led to hold the blessings that are there to be gathered by those who have the eyes to see.

As we embrace the awareness that life itself is seasonal, we are cultivating a spirituality that is sure to sustain us through the long winters ahead. Without even realizing it, we are connecting the circle of life as it should be connected, embracing the profound mystery that the "life-death-life again" cycle is what life itself is really all about.

The work of Mother Earth is finished for another year, and it is time for us to rest as well. We do not have to master the cycles. We only need to go with the flow. With vines picked clean for another year, we seem more able to hear a sacred whisper rising from the earth, letting us know it is time to move on. The hard work of harvest is over. And yet our hearts tell us that the soul work of learning its lessons goes on and on.

Honoring Your Experience

▦ Name some thing you need to let go of. What is preventing you from doing so?

▦ What gifts from the harvest are you holding in your arms this year? Is there something you especially want to give thanks for? Do it now.

▦ What does the tension between gratitude and "letting go" feel like in your life? Give an example.

Reflecting Through Ritual

Take a few moments to be with the small bowl of water and the floating candle. Imagine yourself being carried by the water. Pray for the grace to "go with the flow" of the seasons and cycles of your own life.

Moving Back into Daily Life

A prayer from *Wisdom's Path* by Jan L. Richardson

> That our receiving may be like breathing: taking in, letting go.
> That our holding may be like loving: taking care, setting free.
> That our giving may be like leaving: singing thanks, moving on.

"All Shall Be Well," a song by Kathryn Christian *(Come, Holy Mother* album)

> All shall be well
> All manner of things shall be well.
> (repeat as many times as necessary)

Alternate Ways of Using the Theme with Groups

If you choose to gather in a small group of friends or a large circle, we offer the following suggestions to be adapted to your group's needs and gathering space.

Creating Sacred Space for Your Circle

Dim the lights. Set up a small table draped in colorful fabric in the center of a circle of chairs. Place a lighted candle on it, as well as other symbols that will visually remind your group of the fall season, such as leaves, fruit from the harvest, etc.

Moving Through the Process

Have participants sit around the table. Pass a basket of fall leaves around the circle and invite those gathered to take one as a way of entering into the theme. Invite each woman to introduce herself and share briefly an aspect of letting go that is part of her journey right now or has been recently. Then read the *Slowing Down* reflection and listen to (or sing or read together) the *Going Deeper* song, "The Power of Letting Go." As the group listens to the opening reading and song, have participants reflect on things that they are grateful for.

Summarize the *Reflecting on the Theme* or offer people a few moments to look back over the material quietly. Allow time for personal journaling and reflection before beginning a group conversation. You may use the *Honoring Your Experience* questions to launch the conversation and invite each participant to describe her own journey. Or you can begin by simply asking people to share something about the reflection or theme that spoke to them.

A Ritual to Connect You to Daily Life

Invite participants to stand in the circle and read together the following verse from *Celtic Meditations* by William Farrell: "How patiently the earth carries our footprints, our handprints, all the days of our life. How tenderly she waits for us to come to rest, to sleep within her forever, returning to her the earth we have received from her." Then have someone read the prayer from *Moving Back into Daily Life*. Conclude by singing (or reading together) the mantra "All Shall Be Well."

WINTER: SABBATH

The old, wise Sabbath says: "Stop now. As the
sun touches the horizon, take the hand off the plow,
put down the phone, let the pen rest on the paper,
turn off the computer, leave the mop in the bucket
and the car in the drive….
The deep wisdom embedded in creation
will take care of things for a while.

– from *Sabbath* by Wayne Muller

Creating Sacred Space
Keep it simple! Place a lighted candle and your appointment book or calendar on a table next to you.

Slowing Down
A poem by David Sluyter from the anthology *Prayers for a Thousand Years*

I awoke to the confusion of a new day.
The scraps of dreams, memories of yesterday, and new cravings creeping into awareness.
The sun spilling its light over all but the shadows and a cacophony of sound
from outside and in.
What to make order of? What to let go?
And who makes the choice?
I think I will go down to the river and just watch it flow,
It's been a long time since I have done something really important.

Going Deeper

"Just to Be, " a song by Colleen Fulmer (*Dancing Sophia's Circle* album)

Just to be is a blessing, Just to live is holy.
Just to be, Just to live
Is a blessing, is holy.

Be still and know I am God
In quiet and trust lies your healing
When you look, you'll find me with you.
When you look, you'll find me with you.

So beautiful wild flowers grow
They don't spin, toil, or weave
Yet their smile, delights our God.
Yet their smile, delights our God.

See all the birds of the sky
They don't gather into barns
Yet our God, cares for them.
Yet our God, cares for them.

Asleep on her mother's breast
The child is content and weaned
Oh my soul, trust in our God.
Oh my soul, trust in our God.

Reflecting on the Theme

Take a few moments now to read again the advice "Old, Wise Sabbath" wants to give you in the opening lines of the chapter.

As fall moves into winter, Mother Earth seems to know it is time to let the land lay fallow and go inside for a while. One week moves into another, and the wisdom of the ages calls us to pause. A Jewish woman prays over the Sabbath candles as she lights them. A Muslim chants a call to prayer from the rooftop. A Christian sets out for worship early on a Sunday morning. Together they remind us that there is a time to produce and a time to refrain from producing. Every woman in her own way seems to know that life itself is holy, that there are ancient rhythms of being and doing, resting and working, busyness and stillness that need to be honored. There is wisdom for us that has been buried in the earth and embedded in our religious traditions for centuries. Winter is a time for us to let that wisdom sit with us for a few months.

If we are at all serious about cultivating a spirituality of our own, most of us know we need to get better at taking time, making time, finding ways to treasure the time we have. Yet being overworked, keeping things on schedule, living by our calendars are the perennial challenges that follow us through most of our adult years.

While the familiar words of Jesus beckoning us to come apart and rest a while (see Matthew 11: 28) may ring in our ears, the reality of beginning a day sitting with a cup of coffee and a lighted candle in the quiet of the morning can seem next to impossible. Ours is not a culture that places a lot of value on the interior life, nor does it place a lot of importance on slowing life down. On the contrary, the forces of our society make it very difficult to allow any real quiet time at all. There is the early morning board meeting, the carpool, the unexpected phone call. Once the workday begins, it seldom offers opportunities for us to come apart and rest a while.

There will always be things we must do, responsibilities we must accept. But is there a sacred balance that needs to be reclaimed? As women, can we help one another acknowledge that there is more to life than increasing its speed? Is it okay to say we need time out, that there are limits to our energy, that sometimes it is even important to say no? Can we give ourselves some empty space in a day where we can remember again that we not always in control and that some things have to go on without us? If so, where do we find the courage to begin?

As with most important questions in life, the answer crystallized for Mary Ruth one morning as she was "slaving" over this material around Sabbath:

I had a deadline to meet and was not about to let up until the chapter was finished. As I was driving to work that morning, carrying the weight of the world on my shoulders, I suddenly began smiling. It was a different kind of smile; I was smiling back at a God who was smiling at me. I felt accompanied. It was like being with a friend who knew me through and through and loved me through it all. As with all moments of breakthrough, a flood of memories came tumbling in. First of all, I recalled that the reason behind Sabbath was to help the Jewish people remember that they were led out of slavery into freedom. Sabbath is about liberation, not slavery. Something was definitely wrong with my process. Though I smiled at this epiphany, I also knew it was time for truth-telling: You don't "slave" over Sabbath material. Once I acknowledged that, it was like a Mystery larger than myself sat me down and helped me remember not only the history of Sabbath, but my own more recent history as well.

I recalled going on retreat some years ago, armed with books, journals, agendas and assignments for myself. The night before the retreat began, feeling I still could use one more book to come with me for the week, I visited the local bookstore. As I began to quickly move along the shelf, a person pushed a book a little too far from the other side and another book landed at my feet. It was titled "Don't Just Do Something, Sit There" by Sylvia Boorstein. Needless to say, I was startled; but at some place within myself I knew the book had chosen me. My task for the moment was over, but my ride in the car continued. I was getting the message, but God had sat me down and the conversation was far from over. I had flashbacks of spiritual directors, mentors, friends throughout the years — each present to me at significant moments on my journey, each with the same message: "Don't work at it so hard, let it come." Every time I heard it, it was like I never heard it before, but here in the car, as I heard it again, I felt like I was being shown my own salvation history. It was as if this Wise Old Woman deep inside was letting me hear the wisdom of the centuries: "Stop working at it so hard and take some time out. Slow down. Let it unfold. You're trying too hard. Trust that it doesn't all depend on you. Give yourself a break! Maybe you just need to let go. The answer will come. God is God; Mary Ruth is Mary Ruth."

Clearly the message had taken root, but the ride wasn't over until I sat with one last story. A person I had been seeing for spiritual direction a number of years ago shared an article she had written about her mother's death. At the time, I knew I would never forget it — and clearly I hadn't — but like most things, it got buried underneath the rubble of the noise and busyness of life. Today, it felt like God had scooped it up from my memory bank and handed it back to me.

The story was about this young woman's experience of sitting with her mother during the final year of her life, an experience she referred to in the article as Sabbath. She described how her mother had worked hard at being healthy for nine years after being diagnosed with cancer, but in the tenth year she took a "vacation" from the "work" of healing. Her mother called it her Sabbath. Instead of fighting the disease, she rested. Because of her mother's faith and lifetime of keeping Sabbath, this young woman is able to sit with her mother now and watch her embrace dying with the same guts that she embraced living.

I sat in awe as I remembered every detail of the story. It was as clear to me in the car that day as it was at the first telling. It felt as if it was the pearl of great price Jesus spoke of in Matthew's gospel (see Matthew 13:45), a final fruit of my epiphany as I realized my conversation in the car had ended and the work of the day was about to begin. As I left my car, I was beginning from a different place than I had ended the day before. I felt like Moses wanting to take off his shoes, knowing that these reflections around Sabbath had invited me to walk again on the holy ground of my own life. I knew that somehow this is the invitation extended to us all. Thoreau's "Walden Pond" came to mind, offering me a bit of Sabbath wisdom: "I went to the woods to live deliberately, to front only the essential facts of life…so that when it comes time to die, I will not discover I have not lived. Living is so dear."

Perhaps the greatest gift of Sabbath is that it invites us to pause along the way, in the midst of life and not apart from it. When we cultivate the spiritual practice of honoring it, the routine of life gets interrupted in small intervals — ten minutes, a half hour, maybe even for a day. While it can begin with an early morning walk or sitting by the fire for a few moments at the end of the day, we soon learn it is really about so much more. It is being with our own thoughts, taking time to breathe, just getting off "auto pilot" for a while. To an outsider, it can look as if we are listening to a piece of music, reading a few lines from Scripture, journaling, or momentarily staring into space, but we know it is our way of trying to make room for the Divine Presence to sit with us for a while and help us walk around the holy ground of our own lives. To our surprise, we discover it can happen in a car, a hotel room, a favorite chair, a place of worship, or even in our own backyard.

More often than not, these little Sabbaths allow the stress of the day to fade into the background. They help us remember again that all is gift. They call our attention to what is important and help us begin to see the sacred thread that runs through our ordinary lives. They give us time to process what is unfinished and let go of what we can do nothing about.

Perhaps it is no accident that winter provides a context for these reflections on Sabbath. The stark winter landscape holds some of the great spiritual lessons of the ages:

> *"Go a little slower."*

> *"Remember that you are not in control."*

> *"Give yourself time to trust in what you cannot see."*

For those of us in the North, slowing down in winter becomes a way of life whether we want it that way or not. It takes longer to get dressed in the morning. The car takes time to warm up. We learn to be more tentative about our plans. We walk more slowly, drive more carefully, and are even challenged to cultivate a different kind of seeing if we are to perceive the beauty of a stark winter landscape. These are lessons not all that different from the lessons of Sabbath throughout the ages.

Perhaps the most valuable lesson winter wants to teach us, however, is that new life is stirring beneath the surface, even when everything around us would lead us to believe otherwise. Winter introduces us to the fact that there is a Mystery that calls us to believe in what is not yet apparent. Without ever reading a book or lingering with a theological treatise on the Paschal Mystery, a part of us comes to know that winter will not have the last word, that what seems like the end really isn't. Those little crocuses will soon be knifing their way up through hard ground, and if we are able to pause long enough to notice, we will be equipped to meet the challenges of tomorrow, remembering that there is more to us than ourselves, more to life than what we see.

Years ago, an article by Jean Blomquist in *Weavings* magazine titled "Holy Time, Holy Timing" ended with these words. As you read them, let them become a bit of Sabbath wisdom trickling down through the ages, connecting you with those ancient rhythms and the wisdom they embody — a Jewish woman lighting the Sabbath candles, a Muslim chanting a call to prayer, a Christian setting out for Sunday worship: "Don't try to do it all at once. Take breaks. Build leisure into your journey. Carry plenty of water and drink even when you don't think you are thirsty, because, if neglected, the springs of life within us can dry up without our even knowing it. Eat some of your food now; you need nourishment, and besides, your pack won't be as heavy at journey's end. Watch your step, but more important, stop often and enjoy the view. God is here…. Each moment is holy. All time is God's."

Honoring Your Experience

▨ What are the lessons winter wants to teach you at this point in your life?

▨ Give yourself time to connect with the theme of Sabbath. Stay with whatever is speaking to you, even if it seems outside your normal understanding of Sabbath.

▨ What do you see as some of the benefits for yourself in clearing a space in your day for Sabbath? How might you begin to go about doing so? How do you see this as a spiritual practice?

Moving Back into Daily Life

"The Avowal," a poem from *Oblique Prayers* by Denise Levertov

> As swimmers dare
> to lie face to the sky
> and water bears them,
> as hawks rest upon air
> and air sustains them,
> so would I learn to attain
> freefall, and float
> into Creator Spirit's deep embrace,
> knowing no effort earns
> that all-surrounding grace.

"Lullabye," a song by Cris Williamson, sung by Shaina Noll (*Songs for the Inner Child* album)

> Like a ship in the harbor
> Like a mother and child
> Like a light in the darkness
> I'll hold you a while.
> We'll rock on the water
> I'll cradle you deep
> And I'll hold you while angels
> Sing you to sleep

Alternate Ways of Using the Theme with Groups

> If you choose to gather in a small group of friends or a large circle, we offer the
> following suggestions to be adapted to your group's needs and gathering space.

Creating Sacred Space for Your Circle

Place a small table draped in colorful fabric with two or three white taper candles (or a Jewish menorah if you have one) at the center of a circle of chairs. Set symbols of *time* on the table: an hourglass, alarm clock, appointment book and/or calendar. Also place a small bowl filled with dirt upon it as a symbol of the earth outside lying fallow.

Moving Through the Process

As participants enter the space, invite them to sit around the table. Light the candles or the menorah as a symbol of Sabbath and invite each woman to share a favorite winter memory. Then read the *Slowing Down* reflection and listen to (or sing or read together) the *Going Deeper* song, "Just to Be." As the group listens to the opening reading and song, have each woman remove her watch and reflect on her desire to slow her life down in some way.

Summarize the *Reflecting on the Theme* or offer people a few moments to look back over the material quietly. Allow time for personal journaling and reflection before beginning a group conversation. You may use the *Honoring Your Experience* questions to launch the conversation and invite each participant to describe her own journey. Or you can begin by simply asking people to share something about the reflection or theme that spoke to them.

A Ritual to Connect You to Daily Life

As a way of bringing closure to the session, invite the participants to take a few moments of silence and focus their attention on the symbols in the center of the circle: the small bowl filled with dirt reminding us of the earth lying fallow, the symbols of time illuminated by the candlelight. Then invite the participants to take back the watch they laid down at the beginning of the gathering. Have someone read the poem from *Moving Back into Daily Life*. Conclude by singing (or reading together) the song "Lullabye."

SPRING: GROWING PAINS

My beloved speaks and says to me:
"Arise, my love, my fair one,
and come away;
for now the winter is past,
the rain is over and gone.
The flowers appear on the earth;
the time of singing has come,
and the voice of the turtledove
is heard in our land.
The fig tree puts forth its figs,
and the vines are in blossom.
Arise, my love, my fair one,
and come away."

– Song of Solomon 2:10-13

Creating Sacred Space

Keep it simple! Place a lighted candle and a small clay pot filled with spring soil on a table next to you.

Slowing Down

An excerpt from "Mud Season," a poem from *Selected Poems of May Sarton*

> In early spring, so much a fall of will,
> We struggle through muds of unreason,
> We dig deep into caring and contention;
> The cold unwieldy earth resists the spade.
> But we contend to bring a difficult birth
> Out from the lack of talent, partial scope,
> And every failure of the imagination....

Going Deeper

"God Who Gardens," a song by Colleen Fulmer (*Her Wings Unfurled* album)

> Mother God in whose garden we dwell,
> How beautiful your loving face.
> You desire our holiness and the fruit of the vine,
> We're made in your image and grace.
>
> Let our flowered garden reflect who you are,
> Your passion for wholeness and life,
> Giving us golden sun and the water we need
> To bring us to fullness and life.
>
> Heal our wounds from seasons of pain,
> Touching the roots deep within
> And pruning the branches long withered and dead,
> The ones that no longer give you praise.
>
> Cleanse us, Beloved, with your gentle rains,
> Your love planted firm in our earth,
> Making fertile in us your justice and peace,
> Bringing your beauty to birth.
>
> For you are the God who has called us to life,
> The One who unfolds each brand new day.
> May our being give glory to you, Mother God,
> Your garden is singing your praise.

Reflecting on the Theme

Take a few moments just to be with your own images of spring, especially seeing it as a time of transition between the opposing seasons of winter and summer.

Nowhere is the transition between a long, hard winter and spring's promise of new life more dramatic than in a garden. Winter-weary soil, hard and packed down from the unrelenting elements, begins to soften and yield, ushering in what New Englanders refer to as "mud season" — the unstable time that precedes the budding and beauty of the spring landscape. No longer frozen but not yet fully thawed, the earth is a gooey mess and can repel even the most experienced gardeners. Only the hearty ones, those with vision, know that the garden has something to teach in each of its seasons. So, they are willing to stay with the process and wait out the wisdom the earth will yield over time.

While the garden is an important image and has a rich history in the Christian tradition, it is usually presented to us as a place of respite, a place in which to dwell in beauty or to contemplate the mystery of the earth's seasons and cycles. More recently, however, in the literature of feminine spirituality, some writers have challenged the image of the garden as a place of passive enjoyment. They present it instead as a metaphor for a woman's inner life — suggesting that digging, planting, cultivating and harvesting all speak to the variety of ways we, as women, intentionally tend and care for our spiritual growth. Sherry Ruth Anderson and Patricia Hopkins in *The Feminine Face of God* state it this way: "Just as any plot of soil with seeds and sun and water can become a garden if there is a gardener, so can our lives come to spiritual maturity if we are willing to cultivate them. To cultivate…means to inhabit, to dwell within. Learning how to live the 'daily-ness' of our own lives while opening continually to the sacred seems to take practice — practice in opening, practice in listening, practice in waiting."

Many women agree that the garden is an instructive personal image. Some of us see it as symbolic of the collaborative relationship between ourselves and Mother Earth, of the essential partnership between creature and Creator. We are willing to do our share of the hard work — whatever is required for our flourishing. However, we admit that we need to be able to trust we are not alone in this process. Like the hearty gardeners, we need to believe that there is more to the garden than a muddy field. We need to believe that with commitment and effort some new life will ultimately emerge. Maria Harris makes the connection this way in *Dance of the Spirit*: "Although the earth gives us sustenance and identity, the flowering and fruitfulness of the Garden do not happen unless we tend it and work with it. We are not passive recipients to what it brings. Instead, we are tenders and tillers of the soil, both the soil of the earth and the soil of our own souls. The breadth and length and the depth of our spirituality is, in part, up to us."

If this is so, are we not then all gardeners working the landscape of our lives in every season? Harris' words remind us that before the beauty there is the long list of preparatory chores — the backbreaking labor required to turn over the sleeping earth, the daunting task of working the mud. Muck and mud resist control and make great demands on a gardener, to say nothing of the sheer mess of it all.

Using the lens of feminine spirituality, we can look upon the mud as instructive, a reminder that — both in gardening as well as in our personal lives — transition and change are messy experiences. Navigating both inevitably leaves us feeling somewhat out of control and assures us that we will get at least a little dirt underneath our fingernails.

On the other hand, many of us are also discovering that there is something almost primal about slipping clean hands into the softening spring earth — digging in it, weeding it, planting and transplanting — experiences that bring us closer to the natural rhythms of our own lives. As we work the earth we become immersed in her subtle rhythm, her flourishings and diminishments, her fertility and decay. We begin to see how each phase of gardening has its place in the flow of life and in the growth of everything around us, including ourselves.

Living the seasons and cycles of the garden can be a hopeful reminder to us that the painful places in life, while inevitable, are not the whole story. As we linger with the fullness and decline of the shrubs and plants all around us, we begin to notice how death is just one part of a much larger process.

Our friend Allison found this to be true at a particularly challenging time. She tells the story of having purchased her first home just two months prior to being laid off from her executive position. Because it was autumn and she was starting up her own consulting practice, she decided to economize by postponing any landscaping until spring. With her financial status unchanged by the time spring came, she took upon herself the task of tilling the soggy earth of her vast yard. To say it was rigorous is putting it mildly.

Allison saw the whole ordeal as echoing what felt like the grueling uphill battle she faces every day as a single woman homeowner and entrepreneur "trying to do it all." She was able to stay the course, even when everything around her seemed dull and lifeless, because she knew another cycle inevitably awaited. Each day, as she worked, Allison would take time to visualize in detail an abundant summer garden in full bloom, an image that not only pleased her but empowered her to hang in there with the hard work at hand.

Often we discover it takes a concrete experience to offer us encouragement and support and, as in Allison's case, to invite us to imagine what is still possible as we plod our way through our own muddy seasons of darkness and even despair. In her book *Coming Home to Myself*, Jungian analyst Marion Woodman tells us: "We often associate darkness with negativity, but darkness has…a positive side. Certain things only grow in the dark — babies, dreams, roots…." Yet most of us know it takes extraordinary strength and determination to wait out an extended period of darkness and to trust that it is a "fertile dark" where something new can begin to stir and take shape.

Sarah offers one such example. An effervescent woman, Sarah succumbed to a deep and debilitating depression in late spring. At about the same time she enlisted the help of a professional gardener to upgrade and transplant some shrubs and border plants to brighten both her large yard and her sagging spirits. Earth was turned over to make room for hundreds of bulbs; large plants were moved and went into "shock"; small plants attempted to fill in the gaping holes left in their place. Alas, Sarah's garden was anything but the Eden she had originally envisioned. She waited throughout the growing seasons for her depression to lift and admitted, by autumn, that she still felt entombed — like the bulbs now hiding under so many layers of hardening dirt.

These, and other stories, remind us that there is a mystery — an ancient wisdom — buried in the earth that teaches us over and over again: There is a time to plant, and a time to uproot; a time to bring to birth, and a time to let die (see Ecclesiastes 3:2). When we tap this earthy wisdom we begin to see how life doesn't always accommodate us. Sometimes we are taken places we would rather not go. Loss and limitation, pain and betrayal, disappointments and setbacks, death and dying — all touch each one of us. They are part of every life, just as they are a part of every spiritual tradition. The wisdom of the natural world continually confirms this. Harsh as it seems, living this awareness can bring us to a fertile point and a crucial choice on our spiritual journey: Either we can recoil in anger and disappointment for what might have been or we can open ourselves further to what might yet be.

Faithful gardeners know the wisdom of staying open and close to the earth, trusting that more is in the darkness than what they know, believing in things unseen. Author and educator Parker Palmer seems to affirm this trust when he writes, "The deeper we go into the heart of darkness, the closer we get to the ultimate mystery of God."

As Sarah's story illustrates, it can take a long, long time for signs of life to appear. The wait may feel interminable. Patience wears thin and hope is fragile. Yet frequently it is in the very midst of utter vulnerability and wrenching grief (the heart of darkness?) that something shifts, the ground trembles, the wasteland rejoices and blooms (see Isaiah 35: 2), and life gets stirring once again. To our amazement, a fresh inspiration takes hold or we find the energy to rise up out of all that has held us down. It is a sacred process we share with the natural world: tender shoots of green hope push up through the dark earth, bulbs break open and leave their dried up casings behind, and buds awaken.

Life as we knew it changes dramatically; new life breaks through, unabashed and triumphant. The Buddhists have a saying: "Out of the mud, the lotus blooms." Christians call it the Paschal Mystery. By whatever name we know it, however, as we ponder this phenomenal truth we can't help but wonder: Could it be more than just mere coincidence that the resurrected Jesus chose to appear first to a woman — Mary Magdalene — as she was working her way through a spring garden?

Honoring Your Experience

▨ Give yourself time recall how, like a spring garden, your own experiences of growth and change have been messy or painful and stirred up feelings of insecurity, resistance or fear.

▨ What is the correlation you see between working a garden and going deeper into your inner life? Describe occasions when you have experienced this connection.

▨ Can you recall a time when you felt stuck or mired in indecision? How would you describe the shift from that hard place?

Reflecting Through Ritual

Plant something, anything. If it is spring or summer, plant it outside. If it is fall or winter, plant it in a pot. Water it. Pray over it. Watch it grow. As you do, reflect on your spiritual life and how it reflects the four seasons.

Moving Back into Daily Life

A prayer from *More Than Words* by Pat Kozak, CSJ

Rise up, child of earth,
let life rise up in you,
full term, new born.
Time enough in wondrous darkness,
echoed sounds of voices, stirrings,
splashings of new life.

Relinquish to memory this one mystery
we yearn to know and will again
in after-death.
So much latent still to rise
until our risings lifts us to a depth
that questions every truth
we've ever known.

Mud-stirred of first-clay.
Plaything of a potter who fell
in love with her hand's work.
Blessed be her handiwork.
Blessed be the work of her hands.
Blessed be.

Mud stirred of first sight
of one long since born blind.
So grand an opening to see at last
this mid-life child of multi-colored
song and brilliant dance.
Blessed be.

So much latent
still to see, to dance, to sing
until our rising lifts us to the
depths of that first spring of living
water that spilled us forth in mud and birth.
So long ago and still today.
Blessed we.
Blessed be.

"See Me How I Rise," a song by Marsie Silvestro (*Circling Free* album)

> See me how I rise,
> No more tears in my eyes,
> See me I'm standing oh so strong.
> I am a woman….
>
> I am a woman…
> And I've come to sing, come to sing my song.
>
> And I will restore you,
> And heal your wounds again,
> And you will shine as sunshine does,
> After it's blessed with rain.
>
> Then I will
> Wipe your tears dry,
> And sorrow will be gone,
> And you will sing a new melody,
> And I will be your song….
>
> See me how I rise,
> Nor more tears in my eyes,
> See me I'm standing oh so strong,
> I am a woman…
> I am a woman…
> And I've come to sing, come to sing my song.

Alternate Ways of Using the Theme with Groups

> If you choose to gather in a small group of friends or a large circle, we offer the
> following suggestions to be adapted to your group's needs and gathering space.

Creating Sacred Space for Your Circle

Place a candle, an ordinary clay flower pot filled with soil, a small pitcher of water, and some
garden tools on a table in a circle of chairs. Have a few stems of spring flowers — like daisies or
daffodils — on hand.

Moving Through the Process

As participants enter the space, have them pour a little water into the soil, eventually creating a pot
of mud. Light the candle and invite each woman to choose one of the garden tools to place in front
of her as she shares a favorite spring memory. Then read the *Slowing Down* reflection and listen to
(or sing or read together) the *Going Deeper* song, "God Who Gardens." As the group listens to the
opening reading and song, have each woman reflect on what the words "growing pains" evoke in
them.

Summarize the *Reflecting on the Theme* or offer people a few moments to look back over the material
quietly. Allow time for personal journaling and reflection before beginning a group conversation.
You may use the *Honoring Your Experience* questions to launch the conversation and invite each
participant to describe her own journey. Or you can begin by simply asking people to share
something about the reflection or theme that spoke to them.

A Ritual to Connect You to Daily Life

As a way of bringing closure to the session, invite each woman to approach the pot of mud
individually. Hand each a single flower and invite her to place it in the pot. While the flowers are
being "planted," listen to (or sing or read) the song "See Me How I Rise." At the conclusion of the
song, have participants read the closing prayer from *Moving Back into Daily Life* together, with the
pot full of blooming plants in the middle of the circle.

Part V

WELCOMING THE WATERSHED MOMENTS
Risking the Sacred Journey

THE ART OF PILGRIMAGE

True pilgrimage changes lives
whether we go halfway around the world
or out to our own backyard.

– from *Sacred Journeys* by Martin Palmer

The labyrinth, an ancient spiritual tool, was reintroduced to us as a walking meditation by Lauren Artress, an Episcopalian priest and psychotherapist. She describes the sacred pattern of the labyrinth that she first encountered on the floor of Chartres Cathedral in France dating back to the twelfth century, offering it to us as a metaphor for the spiritual journey. Its forty-by-forty square foot circuitous route (as opposed to the "straight and narrow path") is a pilgrimage experience for all spiritual seekers. The sacred design has been recreated on canvas for others to walk and discover for themselves its power to lead them to the center and out again. Smaller versions of the labyrinth have also been created in order to make it more accessible to all who are seeking spiritual guidance.

Creating Sacred Space

Keep it simple! While at some point you may have the opportunity to actually walk the labyrinth, for now we suggest you imaginatively enter into the experience and place a lighted candle on a small table next to you. Using a finger labyrinth or photograph of a labyrinth or the labyrinth on the previous page, give yourself a few moments to sit with this sacred design and let it symbolize all the twists and turns of your own journey.

Slowing Down

A reading adapted from *Celtic Meditations* by Edward Farrell

> Each person has her own stride. Each person treads the earth distinctively — barefoot and sandals, boots and slippers, work shoes and play shoes, the heaviness and gentleness of feet! The first step of the child and the last step of the dying woman — the Springtime of walking and the Autumn of walking; the Calvary walk and the Ascension walk. All walking is a blessing, a prayer — learning the wisdom of one step at a time, and then daring to take another and still another! Gradually discovering that we are walking, not alone, but together!

Going Deeper

"I Am with You on the Journey," a song by Kathy Sherman, CSJ (*Always with You* album)

> I am with you on the journey and I will never leave you.
> I am with you on the journey, always with you.
> (repeat several times)

Reflecting on the Theme

Take a few moments to imagine your entire life as one long journey with a sacred purpose.

There is a sacred path running through all of life. It begins with our first step and ends with our last. It winds through our homes and places of work. It moves into our churches and back out again. It brings us together with friends and strangers. It twists and turns as we encounter setbacks and disappointments. It does not disappear during times of change and transition. It keeps our feet to the ground as we reach for our dreams and follow our hearts. It rises to meet us as we struggle with difficult decisions, and it often takes us places we never expected to go. As we follow its lead, we get a glimpse of our own spirituality in motion. As we slow down and pay attention, walking itself becomes a way of praying. And moving through our ordinary lives becomes a pilgrimage of its own.

Most of us would hesitate to speak about the journey we are on day by day as a pilgrimage. While the word *pilgrimage* has always been a core metaphor for the Christian life, seldom did it call us to focus on the holy ground of our own lives or leave us with any expectation that God was waiting to be uncovered in the ordinary people and events right around the corner. Instead, on hearing about a pilgrimage we are more apt to imagine a long line of spiritual seekers on their way to a holy shrine or distant site — clearly moving away from daily life, hungry to be taught and guided, and deeply hoping for some kind of inner transformation as they reach their destination.

Since most of us cannot envision such a journey in the near future, subtle messages can leave us feeling that walking a sacred path is something far removed from our own experience. And any thoughts of cultivating spirituality close to home can easily get postponed to a later date — perhaps when the kids are a little older, when the remodeling is done, when the tuition bills are paid, when the work slows down, when the economy picks up. In the process, what we know is most important to us, as well as any kind of prayer and meditation, have a way of getting relegated to some distant future where there will be more time to be reflective, to move a little slower, to listen to our heart's desire, and to follow our own inner compass, wherever we seem to be led.

The problem is that life — with its interruptions and distractions, setbacks and detours, complexities and calamities — goes on, and we end up believing that the sacred path begins and ends somewhere other than where we are. In the process, we are apt to miss the Holy One as she passes by — in the people we are with everyday, the book that falls off the shelf, the sun wanting to set on an old wound, the friend who stays with us through it all, the unexpected courage to do what we have to do, or the child that smiles us back to life at the end of a day.

One thing we know for sure is that daily life is far from a straight and narrow path, nor is spiritual growth easily marked by moving through predictable stages toward some distant goal like those single-focused pilgrims of old. For the most part, life is messy. As women, we are always juggling more than we can handle, and more often than not we feel pressured to be someone other than who we are.

We desperately need new ways of understanding ourselves and the path we are on that can hold up through the more chaotic times. We need fresh images and new ways of praying that can keep us grounded in the present moment and help us accept the ordinary struggles in our daily lives as the heroic struggles of the spiritual life.

Perhaps it is time to learn again the art of pilgrimage — this time not by journeying to some distant site but by allowing the image of the labyrinth to lead us on as we navigate the many twists and turns to our own deep center and back again. Through this walking meditation we can pray with our life experiences as they continue to unfold. Here we can bring the chaos and confusion of the day with us, knowing all that is required of us is that we put one foot in front of the other, learning as we turn and return that the path is there to meet us.

The labyrinth has the power of redefining our journey to God and teaching us the many lessons involved in the art of pilgrimage. Rather than allowing a straight and narrow path to dominate our thinking, we are invited to shift our image to one that is wide and gracious. As we do this, we are reminded that wherever we are at any given moment is precisely where God can best meet us.

While we are grasping blueprints of how life should look five or ten years down the road, this circuitous route of the labyrinth continues to remind us that life is not ours to figure out. Instead we learn to go by going where we have to go, one step at a time.

In fact, sometimes we may find ourselves far from where we had hoped to arrive — praying over an unexpected pregnancy or miscarriage, struggling to forgive or to heal an old wound, trying to accept a situation we can do nothing about, searching for a way to change ourselves or live without the approval of those we love. As we put one foot in front of the other, we gradually come to see that spiritual growth is really about living with our questions, making room for mystery, maybe even hanging on by a thread — all the while knowing that the path itself will hold it all together, hold us together, and lead us on.

The art of pilgrimage continues to call us to cultivate those spiritual practices that can transform an ordinary walk into a sacred path. It can be as simple as taking a walk in our own backyard and capturing the quiet revelations that are all around us. It is training our eyes to see divinity in the little purple crocus knifing its way up through hard ground.

In her book, *Kitchen Table Wisdom*, Rachel Naomi Remen reminds us: "We can see only what we have grown eyes to see. Some of us can only notice miracles. Some of us can only see in times of crisis. Yet we can all learn to see God in the folded sheets." And artist Georgia O'Keefe echoes Remen's thought: "Nobody sees a flower, really — it is so small — we haven't time, and to see takes time, like to have a friend takes time."

The art of pilgrimage is about slowing down and waking up. It is taking to heart the fact that the holy is often hidden and more often than not discovered right beneath our feet: a treasure in the field, a pearl of great price, a mustard seed — each so tiny it could be missed on our way to something else. Pilgrimage is about taking the next steps: dealing now with this illness I'd like to ignore, this decision I'd like to run away from, this phone call I've been avoiding, this stand it is time for me to take. It reminds us that if we are not spiritual in the present moment and where we are, we are not spiritual at all.

Life is a delicate balancing act, kind of like walking in a labyrinth: One day we are on holy ground and we know it; the next day we are out there on the outer rim with no guide in sight. And yet the simple act of walking, when done intentionally, can yield flashes of insight, bring healing energy, plant seeds of wisdom, and show us the way. Perhaps Thich Naht Hahn, a Vietnamese Buddhist monk, captures this insight best when he writes: "Walking on earth is a miracle! We do not have to walk in space or on water to experience a miracle. The real miracle is to be awake in the present moment. Walking on the green earth, we can realize the wonder of being alive."

And so we invite you to continue on your path, ponder the mysteries, notice the miracles, walk the talk, and maybe even take that leap of faith today as you take to heart what the art of pilgrimage is all about: It's the going there, not the getting there, that's important.

Honoring Your Experience

How does the labyrinth or the idea of your own journey as being a "pilgrimage" help you to embrace the daily-ness of your own life in a new way? Give yourself time to reflect on what is speaking to you at this point regarding the sacredness of your own path.

What spiritual practices can help you cultivate the "art of pilgrimage" as you move through the daily-ness of your own life?

Linger with the image of a crocus trying to break through the earth. Does it resonate with your pilgrimage right now or at some time in the past? If so, explain how.

Reflecting Through Ritual

If a finger labyrinth or photograph of a labyrinth is available, give yourself time to move along its path to the center and back out again. (If one is not available, use the labyrinth at the beginning of this chapter.) Let yourself feel gratitude for a moment along the way when you were guided along the labyrinth of your life without quite realizing it.

Moving Back into Daily Life

A reading from *The Art of Pilgrimage* by Phil Cousineau

> The challenge is to learn how to carry over the quality of the journey into your everyday life. The art of pilgrimage is the craft of taking time seriously, elegantly. What every traveler confronts sooner or later is that the way we spend each day of our travel…is the way we spend our lives. Inspired by our journey, perhaps we can learn the "true life" we were searching for is here, where our travels and our home life overlap.

"Long Time Sun," a song by On Wings of Song and Robert Gass (*Songs of Healing* album)

> May the long-time sun shine upon you,
> All love surround you,
> And the pure light within you,
> Guide your way home.
> (repeat three times)

Alternate Ways of Using the Theme with Groups

If you choose to gather in a small group of friends or a large circle, we offer the following suggestions to be adapted to your group's needs and gathering space.

Creating Sacred Space for Your Circle

If you have a finger labyrinth, put it in a visible place in your gathering space. Or if a canvas labyrinth is available, place it on the floor with vigil lights surrounding it or with a single vigil light simply placed in the center.

Moving Through the Process

Have participants join the circle around the labyrinth and trace it with a finger or walk it on the floor. Invite each woman to introduce herself by sharing her experience with any kind of a sacred journey or pilgrimage. Then read the *Slowing Down* reflection and listen to (or sing or read together) the *Going Deeper* song, "I Am with You on the Journey." As the group listens to the opening reading and song, have participants reflect on how their entire lives can be seen as a journey.

Summarize the *Reflecting on the Theme* or offer people a few moments to look back over the material quietly. Allow time for personal journaling and reflection before beginning a group conversation. You may use the *Honoring Your Experience* questions to launch the conversation and invite each participant to describe her own journey. Or you can begin by simply asking people to share something about the reflection or theme that spoke to them.

A Ritual to Connect You to Daily Life

As the group stands in the circle around the labyrinth, have participants silently imagine the twists and turns in their own life and the sacredness of their own path. Then have the group read aloud the reading from *Moving Back into Daily Life*. Conclude by singing (or reading together) the mantra "Long Time Sun."

AWAKENING THE MYSTIC AND PROPHET WITHIN

> Let us imagine that within us is an extremely rich place,
> built entirely of gold and precious stones…
> within us lies something incomparably more precious
> than what we see outside ourselves.
> Let's not imagine that we are hollow inside.
> – from *The Way of Perfection* by Teresa of Avila

Creating Sacred Space

Keep it simple! Place a lighted candle, and a strand of pearls or a few beads on a table next to you.

Slowing Down

A prayer by Mary Ruth Broz, RSM

O Spirit of Life,
You call us to be more
Than we can ask or even imagine.
Help us to uncover
The rich inner life that is ours.
Surprise us with hidden treasures
We never knew we had.
Give us the courage to uncover
A mystic and prophet
Within ourselves.
And show us the way
To bring their wisdom with us
As we struggle to leave
This world a better place.

Going Deeper

"Dig Down Deep," a song by Libby Roderick (*If the World Were My Lover* album)

> Chorus:
> I'm digging way down, down to the bottom of my soul
> I'm digging way down, way down deep
> I'm digging way down, down to the bottom of my soul
> There's clear water running through me
>
> Ain't got no answers, got a whole lot of questions
> And nothing on the surface seems to satisfy me
> Can't find it on the outside, got to feel it on the inside
> And dig down deeper in the mystery.
>
> When terror strikes me in the middle of the night
> And even arms around my body can't comfort me
> My heart is thirsting for that cool drink of water
> Got to pull out my shovel, get busy
>
> Cool, clear water, flowing through me
> Washing all my fears away
> Cool, clear water, flowing through me
> Moving me up, moving me up towards the light of day
>
> When daybreak finds me in the morning light
> And it's hard to hold onto what set me free
> I go down to the river cause it helps me remember
> To dig down deeper in my time of need

Reflecting on the Theme

Give yourself a few moments to take the words that introduce this chapter and imagine the rich inner life that is yours but is often forgotten or neglected in the busyness of your day.

We live in times of unprecedented change. The world we were born into is far different than the one we will be leaving behind. As we women crossed the threshold into a new millennium, many of us knew we were already in the process of ushering in a new era. We felt it in our churches, our world, our relationships with one another and the universe as a whole. Something was over, and something new was trying to unfold.

As women the two of us experienced this on our spiritual journeys as well. Everything began to shift: No single image could any longer define who God is for us; no single religious tradition could carry all wisdom. Nor were we any longer willing to embrace a spirituality that was disconnected from the rest of life or the pressing issues of our times. Life was changing and so were we.

Over the past decades, we have watched the profound difference women have made as they have pioneered creative forms of leadership roles in our churches and hospitals, educational institutions, the corporate world, and spirituality centers of every kind. We never anticipated the profound impact that would come to us as a result of experiencing women preaching and presiding in our places of worship. We never fully grasped how being companioned by another woman in spiritual direction and friendship would have the power to help us know first-hand the feminine touch of God. The groundbreaking work of women scholars and theologians, as well as women musicians and writers, has raised our consciousness regarding the importance of honoring our own experience of the sacred. It has brought freshness to doctrines and dogmas that up until now seemed to have little connection with life as we were being called to live it.

Clearly, our hearts have been stirred by those who have not been afraid to pay the price that change demands. However, we know the work that has begun is far from finished. We still continue to witness the pain of women whose gifts cannot find a place in the churches they have loved and worked in all their lives. We experience our own demons of discouragement and powerlessness as we witness the injustice and oppression of women that continues to permeate every segment of our society and is found in so many faces of human suffering around the world. In the midst of it all, however, our hope lies in those who are staying in the struggle for the long haul and are not about to be deterred from the work that must be done. These heroes and heroines inspire us as they work tirelessly to relieve human suffering, live lives of compassion, and foster dialogue around issues of sexuality, politics, and a sustainable future for our planet.

Now, more than ever, the world needs all of us to be wiser people. But the wisdom we need is not easily available to us in newspapers, on television, or over the Internet. It is the kind of wisdom that comes with paying attention to the quality of our interior life — to who we are becoming in the midst of all we are doing. When we are faced with hard decisions, it is the kind of wisdom that challenges us to move away from our desks and the busyness of life and give ourselves time to pause, reflect, pray — and sometimes to even stop and smell the flowers! As we slow life down in these simple ways, we begin to discover that often we have our own best answers planted deep within us by a larger Mystery that has been with us all along. In a similar way, on our return to work we seem more able to tap into the imagination and creativity necessary to face the challenges that come with raising families, doing business, and even knowing where we stand regarding the critical issues of our times.

"Let us imagine that within us is an extremely rich place, built entirely of gold and precious stones… within us lies something incomparably more precious than what we see outside ourselves. Let's not imagine that we are hollow inside." These words of Teresa of Avila need to be taken to heart. They poetically challenge us to re-imagine who we are as they describe the rich inner resources that await us if we are willing to go deep enough. They dispel the feelings of inadequacy and self-doubt that too often plague us and remind us that we have each been given gifts that are needed now more than ever to move life forward and leave this world a better place.

Meister Eckhart once described all of spirituality as "waking up" — going through life "awake" and not asleep. Perhaps this advice can serve us well not only on the outer journey but on the inner one as well. There is more to us than we know. There is a rich heritage we have yet to claim — a wisdom that comes as we learn more about the mystics and prophets who went before us and begin to recognize that they live within us as well.

While we have all had mystical and prophetic moments in our everyday lives — whether we notice them or not — few of us use such lofty language to describe the experiences and may not even see the importance of doing so. Yet the great spiritual figures from our tradition seem to carry an important key to the future, and making a connection with them may unlock some hidden treasures that can empower us for the work that is ours.

To awaken the mystic within is to trust the God of our ordinary experience, to no longer be content with a spirituality built solely on what others tell us about the holy. The mystic who resides inside each of us knows there is a gift-dimension to human life and no one can take that "inner knowing" away from us. When we uncover the mystic within, we begin to find ourselves mysteriously connected to the suffering around us, in awe as we watch a child hovering over an ant-hill, stretched to our core as we witness friends rise up after times of loss and illness. To journey with the inner mystic is to feel an invisible arm around ourselves as we struggle to find our voice and speak our truth.

Sometimes this inner mystic comes in a fleeting moment when our hearts are weary and our hope grows thin, but more often than not, she quietly accompanies us in our daily lives, keeping us alert to the fact that God is here in all the joys and sorrows. Often she leaves us with a sense of being one with all of creation, being connected in ways we never could have imagined, being aware of a God so much bigger than we ever envisioned. These kinds of moments happen more than we realize, but without an awakened consciousness — without the imagination to draw upon the rich inner life that is ours — they often go unnoticed and we go forth unchanged.

On the other hand, when we do pay attention to our inner voice, these kind of moments have the power to change forever the ways we view ourselves, our relationships with one another, and the universe itself. It is the mystic within us who wakes us up and slows us down!

Mysticism is hard to define. The poet Rainer Maria Rilke once wrote: "The work of the eyes is done…now go and do heart work." Heart work is what mystics do well. At some point, they come to trust that what they hear on the inside is as important as what they hear on the outside. They will not be intimidated. They know that the holy lives in them, that God speaks directly to them, and that they will not be alone as they set out to do what they feel called to do.

Mystics include people like Julian of Norwich, Hildegarde of Bingen, Catherine of Siena, Etty Hillesum, Gandhi, Rumi: spiritual seekers from every religious tradition who knew that the old way of doing things was no longer working, who were not afraid to speak in the light what they heard in the dark. They entered the mystery of life and could not contain what they experienced; they learned from the earth and its seasons; they cried out for justice and called for reforms of every kind. They are known as mystics, but in truth they are prophets as well. As Joan Chittister explains, "The prophet is simply the mystic in action."

The prophet is that part of us that is willing to speak the truth in love. She helps us to give voice to what we know in our hearts. She is not afraid to live out of her deeper, truer self. She knows there is a cost to challenging systems that have been in place for centuries, and yet she is even more aware that there is a greater cost in keeping silent.

These wonderful words "mystic and prophet" are not only embodied in those we admire from afar but live inside us as well. As Thomas Merton wrote, "This true inner self must be drawn up like a jewel from the bottom of the sea…." Only then — when we are conscious of the rich inner resources that are ours — will we come to trust that our lives are meant to be a blessing and find comfort in knowing that there is a wise and contemplative spirit within that wants to accompany us as we give birth to the person we truly are.

Clearly, we can no longer settle for a way of being spiritual that would have us believe we are hollow inside. Like Teresa of Avila, let us imagine that within us is an extremely rich palace, a world built entirely of gold and precious stones, a place where head and heart mentor one another and intuition and imagination find their rightful place next to logic and all that is rational. Here action and contemplation no longer need to be experienced as separate roads on our spiritual journey.

The mystic and prophet *together* can give shape to new ways of being human, being church, and being a spiritual presence in the world around us.

Honoring Your Experience

What is your response to hearing there is a mystic and prophet within you? If you embraced the mystic and prophet within yourself, what do you feel they have to offer? How would you act differently?

Is there "heart work" you are feeling called to do at this time? Describe it as best you can.

What are some ways you see the old order crumbling and something new wanting to come forth?

Reflecting Through Ritual

Close your eyes. Imagine yourself as one of the great mystics and prophets in history. What century would you have lived in? What country? What would have been your message? As you return to your daily life, what do you want to say to the mystic and prophet within you?

Moving Back into Daily Life

"Transform My Gratitude into Courage," a poem from *My Heart in My Mouth* by Ted Loder

> Make us bold and visionary enough
> to measure our lives not so much
> by victories won or successes achieved
> but by worthy battles engaged,
> scars of faith endured,
> noble comrades joined.

"Keep On, Strong Heart," a song by Libby Roderick (*If the World Were My Lover* album)

I know you're tired, I know you're weary
I know you want to give up some days
Some days are so hard, some days are too lonely
But I love you so and there's no other way.

Chorus:
So keep on strong heart, don't fail me now
We must keep going a little bit longer
Keep on strong heart, I know somehow
That you will be there when the great new day dawns.

Oh you have been toiling what seems like forever
Sometimes you feel you're right where you began
Your mind starts to ache, your body it trembles
It's only your heart that tells you can.

And the fight will go on, we're talking about freedom
We can so we must and we must so we dare
If your body gives way, I will carry you homeward
When that new day dawns, my love, you will be there.

And if you need courage, I'm right here beside you
And if I need strength, I will look in your eyes.
And the fight will go on, we're talking about freedom.

So keep on strong heart, don't fail me now
We must keep going a little bit longer
Keep on strong heart, I know somehow
That we will be there when the great new day dawns
That we will be there when the great new day dawns
That we will be there when the great new day dawns
Yes we will be there when the great new day dawns.

Alternate Ways of Using the Theme with Groups

If you choose to gather in a small group of friends or a large circle, we offer the following suggestions to be adapted to your group's needs and gathering space.

Creating Sacred Space for Your Circle

Place some colorful fabric on a table along with a candle and a small bowl of pearls or beads, symbolic of the riches we all have inside ourselves. Scatter books featuring the lives of mystics and prophets on the table.

Moving Through the Process

Light the candle and have participants join the circle around the table. Have each of them pick up one of the books on mystics and prophets. Invite each woman to introduce herself by naming a mystic or prophet that she admires, either from history or today, and telling why. Then read the *Slowing Down* reflection and listen to (or sing or read together) the *Going Deeper* song, "Dig Down Deep." As the group listens to the opening reading and song, have participants reflect on their own inner strengths.

Summarize the *Reflecting on the Theme* or offer people a few moments to look back over the material quietly. Allow time for personal journaling and reflection before beginning a group conversation. You may use the *Honoring Your Experience* questions to launch the conversation and invite each participant to describe her own journey. Or you can begin by simply asking people to share something about the reflection or theme that spoke to them.

A Ritual to Connect You to Daily Life

Pass the bowl around and have each member of the group choose a pearl or bead. Tell them to take it with them as a symbol of the rich inner life in them that is waiting to be discovered and to put it in a place in their home or work where they will notice it. Then have the group read aloud the poem from *Moving Back into Daily Life*. Conclude by singing (or reading together) the song "Keep On, Strong Heart."

THE COSMIC WALK

Why did you give us such tender skin
and ask us to carry fire?

– from *Night Visions* by Jan L. Richardson

Creating Sacred Space

Keep it simple! Place a photograph of the Earth taken from the moon (or some other photo of the cosmos) next to you. Put a lighted candle on a small table next to it.

Slowing Down

"The Cosmic Walk" as developed by Sister Miriam Therese McGillis

The Cosmic Walk is a walking meditation that offers us a glimpse into our sacred origins. While there are many creation stories, this one is an attempt to connect the work of scientists from around the world with the on-going spiritual search we have to better understand who we are and how we came to be. It is the unfolding story of the universe, the story of life on earth, and the story of our personal history as a human community. This time of prayer is an invitation to enter into the vast mystery of creation that has been at work for thirteen billion years, and to help you experience the awe and wonder of life as you know it today. We invite you to imaginatively enter into the experience by quietly reading the sequence of events that comprise the walk itself:

> *"In the beginning was the dream, the dream was with God and the dream was God. The dream was with God in the Beginning. Through the dream all things came to be, not one thing had its being but through the dream; and out of this, Mystery created light or light came forth."– adapted by Thomas Berry from the prologue of John's gospel*

13.7 billion years ago, the universe was dreamed into being

12.7 billion years ago, the galaxies and stars formed

4.6 billion years ago, our grandmother star collapsed into our supernova

4.5 billion years ago, the sun, solar system, and planet Earth were born out of stardust

4 billion years ago, in the emergence of simple bacteria, the Earth awakened into life

2 billion years ago, oxygen formed in the atmosphere

1 billion years ago, life was mysteriously drawn toward union, and the complex organisms learned to reproduce sexually

510 million years ago, the first fish moved through the oceans

410 million years ago, the first land plants appeared

395 million years ago, the first insects appeared

215 million years ago, the first mammals evolved

150 million years ago, the first birds took flight through the air and Earth broke into song

120 million years ago, the first flowers appeared on the land

40 million years ago, the dinosaurs disappeared

3.3 million years ago, the great ice ages of the Earth began

60,000 thousand years ago, modern "homo sapiens" emerged in the unfolding life process

10 thousand years ago, the end of the last ice age, the beginning of agriculture, and the rise of the great civilizations of humankind

3,200 years ago, the Exodus of Israel from Egypt

2,500 years ago, the teachings of Confucius and the Buddha flourished throughout India and China

2,300 years ago, Classic Mayan civilization flourished in the Americas

2,000 years ago, Jesus — a Dream of God — revealed his teachings of unity and spread the message throughout Judea and Galilee

1,400 years ago, the teachings of Mohammed and Koran spread throughout Africa, Asia, and southern Europe

65 years ago, humans discovered an expanding universe and split open the atom

36 years ago, humans — on a journey to the moon — turned around and saw Earth as a whole for the first time

Today, all humans can know the common story of their origin

At this very moment, a baby is being born. How will we pass on the story?

Going Deeper

"Ground of All Being," a song by Jan Novotka (*Melodies of the Universe* album)

> Ground of All Being
> Breath of All Life
> Spirit within all things
> Open our eyes,
> Open our ears,
> Stir in our hearts,
> Awaken our minds,
> And then we will bend low
> And then we will know
> That all is holy, all is one
> All is holy, Holy One.

Reflecting on the Theme

Take a few moments to imagine yourself contemplating your sacred origins with all of creation.

M ary Ruth experienced the Cosmic Walk as one of those "watershed moments" in her life that has had a way of redefining who she is:

The Cosmic Walk not only changed me but also changed how I have come to view everything around myself. As I set out to reflect upon this ritual, I invite you to make the journey with me — either by reading it again in the "Slowing Down" section or by going on the walk itself as I did.

When I first embarked upon the Cosmic Walk, I thought I was being invited to join with others in a walking meditation not all that different from those I had taken part in over the years. I welcomed it as a time to slow down, to be mindful of the present moment and the holy ground we walk upon. But as I began the walk that night, I felt as if I had stumbled into "a night different from all the others," as Jewish people describe the Passover at their Seder meal. This walk was about our sacred origins and how we as humans came to be who we are as the universe unfolded over time. While at first the Cosmic Walk can seem disconnected from ordinary life, I soon discovered it was not. A string of yarn was lying on the floor marking the path we were to follow. Vigil lights marked significant moments in our evolution.

Approximately twenty signs lay on the floor, carefully placed next to each light, trying to give words to thirteen billion years of creativity. Music played in the background, and a "New Story" — our story — was being told beneath our feet. We were invited to walk quietly, reverently, and to listen attentively. I soon found myself marveling at what I heard.

The Cosmic Walk begins where God began — with the very first act of creation. Some refer to this as "the big bang"; others have described it as "the great birth." I could feel the sacred push of creative energy moving me along a path that had a life of its own. Looking down, I began to read: thirteen billion years ago, the universe came into being; twelve billion years ago, the galaxies were formed and stars exploded. I continued to walk while the story unfolded: four and a half billion years ago, the sun formed; four billion years ago, the earth awakened into life. Millions of years passed and the story went on. Fish, plants, animals, flowers, dinosaurs, birds each emerging at a given moment. Finally, less than 100,000 years ago, we as a human species appeared. How could one not be amazed at how new we were to this community of life and the story that had been unfolding before our eyes?

As I continued to reflect upon the experience, I was able to recognize some of the shifts that were going on within me. While at the beginning I was eager to learn about something I had only vaguely heard about, I knew I certainly wasn't prepared for the awesomeness of the experience. For a brief moment, I could actually feel science and spirituality becoming one and the same path. In a similar way, my head and heart joined together — not competing for my attention but grounding me in ways I never anticipated. Walking, processing, imagining the scope of creation, taking in the unfathomable mystery that set it all in motion, suddenly left me knowing in my bones that I was connected to all that had come before and all that would come after.

As I walked, I was able to watch the process unfold, conscious of how creative and surprising and sacred it began to feel. For billions of years, life was going on without us. One species was accommodating another; old forms were giving way to the new. Life was making room for more life, and diversity was enriching rather than threatening. Suddenly I was beginning to feel embraced by the intimacy of my surroundings. Nothing was separate. Everything was dependent on everything else. This is the web of life, and we as humans are woven into it.

Following the yarn on the floor, it became clear to me that a sacred thread runs through it all. There is more to life than what appears on the surface. There is a Cosmic Mystery — recognized by scientists and mystics alike — that penetrates everyone and everything. Perhaps that is why Pierre Teilhard de Chardin referred to this world as the "Divine Milieu" and why St. Ignatius of Loyola would name the goal of the Spiritual Exercises as "Finding God in All Things." Suddenly I realized that the same Spirit has been with us since the beginning of time, a spirit that is feminine in her nurturing generosity. No wonder we hear about her hovering over creation in the Book of Genesis and are reminded again of her coming on the Feast of Pentecost. It is this same Spirit — the spark of the divine — that has been in everyone and everything since the beginning of time: wood, rock, water, fire, the plant I'm watering, the earth I'm standing upon, the little dog I'm walking. Grace is everywhere, and everything is holy. As humans, we must take our place in the circle of life. We are clearly not the center of the universe.

As the walk continued, I began to see that we humans are the beneficiaries of all that has gone before. At first, it took me by surprise how late in the evolutionary process the appearance of Jesus was. However, in his book "Jesus and the Reign of God," C.S. Song offers us this perspective: "Strictly speaking, Jesus did not bring God's reign into the world, for it was already there. What he did was to engage people in the manifestation of it, to enable them to know it is there, and to open their mind's eye to see it."

Reflecting on these words, it seems to me that Jesus embodies the best that we can still become. He showed us how we might take our place in the sacred process of evolution. He was not afraid to insist on the spirit of the law, to reach out to those who were excluded, to listen for wisdom from the lilies of the field and the birds of the air. He went about showing us that human life is about living a life of love and relieving human suffering in whatever ways we are able. He not only showed us the way to be fully human but also reminded us that we have the capacity to do even greater things than he accomplished (see John 14:12).

Yet Jesus' invitation was not easily grasped in his time, nor is it today. We need a new consciousness of what it means to be human. We ourselves are in process. As a human species, we are young. Some even describe us as rebellious adolescents who find it hard to go with the flow. One thing we know for sure is that we have a lot to learn. We stand. We fall. We remember. We forget. We have not yet fully evolved.

And so, as I found myself taking those final steps on the path set out for us, I was reminded of the tremendous power we have and the choices that still lie ahead. The final piece of the story reminds us that within the past hundred years alone we as humans have discovered our own potential for good and for evil. We have discovered we are capable of standing on the moon and splitting the atom. But we also know we are capable of the holocaust and of destroying life — even the planet itself — with the choices we make. My walk was temporarily at its end, but I realized that we are not at the end of the complete story. There is an Ancient Love that is still guiding our way.

As we all continue to walk the Cosmic Walk, life pushes forward beneath our feet. A baby is being born at this very moment. Will we tell her the whole story? Will she come to know her place in the sacred community of life or will she — like most of us — come to see herself as disconnected, separate, on her own? Will she come to know that how she walks upon this earth really matters, not only for all who will come after her but for all that has gone before her as well? Will she come to really understand that the universe itself has spent thirteen *billion* years preparing for her arrival? Will she really understand that she is at the leading edge of creative development, and will she lead us further along that path?

We ourselves are literally stardust, they say. If so, our light hovers in a dark sky. There is fire in our bones. We were made to take our place in the circle of life. When we do, we will know we have been part of birthing a future worthy of passing on, one now almost ready to be named.

Honoring Your Experience

- We as humans are obviously relative newcomers to creation. What impact does that awareness have on you?

- If there is one contribution you would like to make to the Cosmic Walk, what would it be?

- As a result of taking the Cosmic Walk, what are some of the insights you want to pass on to the next generation?

Reflecting Through Ritual

Take a chair into your backyard or pull it up to a window with a clear view of the sky. Gaze at the moon and the stars and try to imagine their distance and age. Now imagine yourself as a piece of stardust — not an insignificant piece but perhaps the most important piece in the Cosmic Walk. Pray for the creative spirit of the feminine face of God to come over you and bless you as you continue the journey of creation.

Moving Back into Daily Life

A poem from *Night Visions* by Jan L. Richardson

Why did you give us
Such tender skin
And ask us
To carry fire?

We are consumed
By our own smoldering,
Hardly knowing
The power we carry
To scald.

Dress the wounds
We have borne
And given
From our own burning.

Make us wise
To the fire in our bones,
That it may be
For warmth and light in
All our darkness.

"This Ancient Love," a song by Carolyn McDade (*This Ancient Love* album)

Long before the night was born from darkness
Long before the dawn rolled unsteady from fire
Long before she wrapped her scarlet arm around the hills
There was a love
This ancient love was born.

Long before the grass spotted green the bare hillside
Long before a wing unfolded to wind
Long before she wrapped her long blue arm around the sea
There was a love
This ancient love was born.

Long before a chain was forged from the hillside
Long before a voice uttered freedom's cry
Long before she wrapped her bleeding arms around a child
There was a love
This ancient love was born.

Long before the name of a God was spoken
Long before a cross was nailed from a tree
Long before she laid her arms of colors 'cross the sky
There was a love
This ancient love was born.

Wakeful our night, slumbers our morning
Stubborn the grass sowing green wounded hills
As we wrap our healing arms to hold what her arms held
This ancient love, this aching love
Rolls on.

Alternate Ways of Using the Theme with Groups

If you choose to gather in a small group of friends or a large circle, we offer the following suggestions to be adapted to your group's needs and gathering space.

Creating Sacred Space for Your Circle

Create your circle outside or at least near a window. If it is evening, dim the lights and light a candle. Place a photograph of the Earth taken from the moon in a visible place. If you have the room, build your own primitive version of the Cosmic Walk. Place a piece of bright-colored yarn (approximately forty yards long) on the floor in the shape of a spiral moving outward. Be sure to allow room for participants to walk along its path. On small pieces of cardstock, label the major cosmic events (see the *Slowing Down* section) and place them along the yarn with a vigil light on the floor next to each one. Place the cards in such a way that one is able to get a sense of the relative time between each event, with the "big bang" at the center and moving outward to today. (Note: If room is not available to do the Cosmic Walk, a miniature version can be constructed on a table in the middle of a circle of chairs.)

Moving Through the Process

As participants arrive, light the candles and have participants sit in silence around the Cosmic Walk. Before anyone introduces themselves, read the description of the Cosmic Walk from the *Slowing Down* section. Then have the participants walk the Cosmic Walk or imagine themselves doing so while they listen to (or sing or read together) the *Going Deeper* song, "Ground of All Being." After everyone is done with the Cosmic Walk, have each participant introduce herself and give her initial reactions.

Summarize the *Reflecting on the Theme* or offer people a few moments to look back over the material quietly. Allow time for personal journaling and reflection before beginning a group conversation. You may use the *Honoring Your Experience* questions to launch the conversation and invite each participant to describe her own journey. Or you can begin by simply asking people to share something about the reflection or theme that spoke to them.

A Ritual to Connect You to Daily Life

As your time comes to an end — especially if this is the last session that the group will do together, at least for a while — have each woman share what this process has meant to them and how it will change how they act. Then have everyone join hands around the Cosmic Walk, close their eyes, and imagine that they are moving into the future together. At this point, ask each woman to name one hope she has for that future with a single word or phrase. Finally, have the group read aloud the poem from *Moving Back into Daily Life* and conclude by singing (or reading together) the song "This Ancient Love."

A book like this is necessarily unfinished, but the "birthing waters" surround us everywhere. Womanriver is flowing on. One thing the two of us have come to know is that we are not alone as the work of unprecedented change goes on. This simple truth came to us some years ago in the writings of the thirteenth-century mystic, Meister Eckhart: "God is a great underground river that no one can dam up and no one can stop."

This image of the sacred is one we continue to cling to, one that has reassured us over and over again that we are all part of a much larger mystery that is leading the way. It is this great underground river — this mystery of life — that we believe not only brought the two of us together but also led us to birth Wellstreams, a center of feminine spirituality, where together with hundreds of other women we learned the art of spiritual midwifery.

It is there that we learned the importance of women's friendships and how essential they are in helping all of us trust our own experience and honor the holy ground of our own lives. While we initially thought we were beginning a center to help others uncover the sacred in their ordinary lives, we had no idea the impact those circles and our own spiritual direction practices would have upon us personally. While these pages give testimony to our own growth, one example poignantly stands out in our minds.

A few years ago, while lamenting the tremendous changes taking place all around us — terrorism, scandals, the ongoing oppression of women worldwide — a mutual friend of ours named a reality neither of us had yet put into words: **"Maybe things have to crumble before something new can emerge."** In that moment, we somehow realized that what seems like the end really isn't. The institutions around us may be crumbling, but we are constantly being challenged to listen for the groans of birth in the midst of the chaos.

This book is our attempt to invite you to do the same. Though much we have all cherished is dying, the cries of new life are all around:

- in women who are making choices to seek one another out in retreats, book clubs, over lunch, in spirituality circles, and around kitchen tables everywhere;

- in those who are making room for daily spiritual practices in their busy lives — taking a walk, lighting a candle, journaling, meditating, and inspiring others to do the same;

- in those who are willing to ask the hard questions around sexuality and gender;

- in those who refuse to be silenced and are finding ways to support and bless one another even when our church communities are not ready to do the same;

- in those who are tirelessly working on the front lines of change;

- in those who are courageously giving voice to their values in their personal relationships, homes and churches, organizations and institutions;

- in the leaders of our church communities who continue to foster dialogue and a spirit of open-mindedness around difficult and controversial issues;

- in old women and young women, women from all lifestyles and religious traditions;

- in the men who share with us a vision of mutuality and partnership.

All of you make us aware that the visions and dreams we carry are bigger than any of our individual issues and that our task as midwives is to facilitate a safe delivery of a spirituality worth passing on. In writing this book we came to experience the role of midwife in a very real way. From the beginning this effort has been a collaboration. Each time one of us hit a bump in the road along our creative path, the other was there to prod, encourage and even challenge. We were also able to celebrate together each time a piece of the project came together or we uncovered just the right story or poem or music to enhance a particular theme. For months we lived and breathed this project, and today we breathe a sigh of delight as we pass on the fruit of our labor for your reflection.

Spirituality centers will come and go. Churches will open and close. Wise women will come into each of our lives and move on. But when we feel most alone and question whether anything has changed at all, the words of Eckhart will lead us on: "God is a great underground river that no one can dam up and no one can stop."

So the journey continues. While we stand on the shoulders of many great women who have gone before us, we also feel a responsibility for those who will follow after us. We want them to know there is a spirit working in them that can do infinitely more than we can ask or even imagine (see Ephesians 3:20). For that to happen, we all need to get ourselves to places where living water flows. We need to keep the conversation going; speak our truth; trust our inner wisdom; listen to our bodies; connect to the seasons and cycles of the earth. We need to stay awake; pay attention; dig down deeper; and simply breathe. We need to leave room for mystery; honor our questions; and, perhaps most importantly, be willing to pay the price to see our visions and dreams come true.

We are all midwives of an unnamed future. We never know when the day or the hour will come when the future we have been birthing will break through and be ready to be named. But even as we say that, we realize that this birth is not only something that will occur in the distant future. Change is in the air we breathe. The time is now. The water is breaking and the midwives are here. New life is crowning. Womanriver is flowing on.

As you continue on your own path, we offer you the words to the song "Womanriver Flowing On" by Carol (Etzler) Eagleheart to accompany you along the way:

> Womanriver flowing on
> Womanriver flowing on and on
> Womanriver flowing on and on
> Womanriver flowing on.
>
> Womanriver, how you come with me
> Flowing on through every century
> Flowing on to what is yet to be
> Womanriver flowing on.

Womanriver flowing on
Womanriver flowing on and on
Womanriver flowing on and on
Womanriver flowing on.

Womanriver flowing free
I hear you moving in the heart of me
Fillin,' touchin' every part of me
Womanriver flowing on....

IN GRATITUDE

Midwives of an Unnamed Future has been from the outset a collaborative effort between the two of us. Because of the stories and reflections that have contributed to its birth, however, many others have midwived its development, and we take this opportunity to mention some of them.

We are indebted first of all to those women who have been sharing their lives so personally with each of us for more than twenty years as they have sat with each of us in spiritual direction, on retreats, and especially in the circles that gathered at Wellstreams — a center of feminine spirituality we founded in 1991. Because of them, we have learned first-hand that there is a resiliency to the human spirit and have arrived at a place in our own lives where we can speak with confidence about the cycles and seasons of women's lives and the Sacred Thread that runs through all of them.

Secondly, we are grateful to those women-friends who believed that the work of Wellstreams was meant to be shared with a larger circle and never stopped encouraging us to do so. Thanks to all of you who believed this book into existence by your financial support: The Sisters of Mercy, Anita Banas, Joan Bransfield, Jack and Sally Daniels, Madeleva Deegan, Audrey Denecke, Tina Malnati, Kitty Nagler, Carolotta Oberzut, Bonnie Rendl, Joe Ruiz, Cathy and Mike Schack, Jane Schlosser, Barbara Stafford, and Jane Tompkins.

A turning point came to us the day Greg Pierce, president and co-publisher of ACTA Publications, called us up after receiving a few chapters of our manuscript and bravely supported the project by becoming the publisher and editor of this book, with help from Nicole Kramer, Patricia Lynch, Jamie Pilloni, and the rest of his staff. We are deeply grateful to him for recognizing the need for a book such as this and believing in us as first-time writers.

Our special appreciation to Jean Clough, who brought her expertise as a photographer to our project, intuiting how her gift could enhance our own reflections.

We also owe much to those who read pieces of the manuscript along the way and shared their experience and expertise with us at critical moments: Mary Beth Sammons, Mary Garzino, Jane Tompkins, Avis Clendenen, and Barbara Stafford.

Then there are Louise Gates, Sally Daniels, and the women who gathered with us month after month over lunch in a boardroom at the Sanchez and Daniels law offices in downtown Chicago. We want you to know that your commitment to deepen your own spirituality and your willingness to reflect with us on your lives as women on a spiritual journey kept our feet planted on holy ground and continued to confirm for us the work we were about.

As the manuscript unfolded, we learned how influenced we have been by those who have inspired us. To those poets and musicians, theologians, artists, and writers who have left us with fresh images and symbols that rose out of the Sacred Feminine, we are grateful. Because of you, the birthing process was eased. You planted the seeds we were able to expand upon and stirred our passion for a feminine spirituality.

Nor will we forget those who worked securing permissions, making phone calls, and assisting us in countless ways. A special thanks to Ethel Detz, OP, Julie Berggren, and Peggy Drennan — who readily responded to our need for help and whose contributions made this book possible in very concrete ways.

We are, of course, grateful for our families and close friends who stood by us every inch of the way. We never anticipated the perils of a writer's life and are forever grateful to those who nudged us on with a sense of humor, a grain of truth, and an unswerving belief that this too will pass! Although we can name only a few here, we know we are deeply blessed by many. For now, we simply acknowledge Mad and Laurette, who on a daily basis never seemed to tire of finding new ways of asking how the book is coming, and Mike and Joe, for being there always and for sharing with wit and wisdom their belief in this project and in us.

All of you — and many others who will go unnamed — have helped us better understand the importance of midwives in bringing dreams to birth. This book clearly is the work of so many. As you read along, we know many of you recognized yourselves in these pages, even though we may have hidden you in our own words, given you another name, gleaned your wisdom and made it our own.

Finally, for all of you readers, and for the many ways you continue to give shape to a spirituality worthy of passing on, we say thank you.

WITH PERMISSION

Many books, articles, poems and songs provided inspiration for *Midwives of an Unnamed Future*. Extensive quotes were used with permission as noted below, others were determined to be in the public domain or fair use. The authors have made every effort to trace the ownership of all copyrighted materials found in this book and to make full acknowledgment for their use. Omissions brought to our attention will be corrected in a subsequent edition.

Midwives of an Unnamed Future

Excerpt from "A Psalm for Midwives," from *WomanWitness* by Miriam Therese Winter. Copyright © 1992 by the Medical Mission Sisters. Reprinted by permission of Miriam Therese Winter.

Excerpt from *Blessings: A WomanChrist Reflection on the Beatitudes* by Christin Lore Weber. Copyright © 1989 by Christin Lore Weber. Reprinted by permission of the author.

"May You Walk," from *On the Other Side* by Marsie Silvestro. Copyright © 1993 by Marsie Silvestro. Reprinted with permission.

"I Am with You on the Journey," by Kathy Sherman, CSJ, from her recording *Always With You*. Reprinted with permission, courtesy of www.ministryofthearts.org.

Daring Pioneers Redefining Holiness

"Standing on the Shoulders," the official theme song of the 75th Anniversary of Women's Suffrage honoring the 19th Amendment to the Constitution, by Joyce Johnson Rouse, recorded by Earth Mama® on *Love Large*. Copyright © 1995 by Rouse House Music (ASCAP). Available at www.earthmama.org. All rights reserved.

Excerpt from *In Wisdom's Path: Discovering the Sacred in Every Season* by Jan L. Richardson. Copyright © 2000 by Jan L. Richardson, published by The Pilgrim's Press. Reprinted by permission of Jan L. Richardson.

"Standing Before Us" by Carole (Etzler) Eagleheart. Copyright © by Carole (Etzler) Eagleheart from the recording *Thirteen Ships*. Reprinted by permission of Carole (Etzler) Eagleheart.

Partners in a Process of Change

Gathering the Fragments

Spinning a Finely Textured Life

Becoming Bread

Excerpt from *Sacred Journeys: A Woman's Book of Daily Prayer* by Jan L. Richardson. Copyright © 1995 by Jan L. Richardson. Used by permission of Upper Room Books.

Excerpt from "Blessing the Bread: A Litany," by Carter Hayward from *Our Passion for Justice: Images of Power, Sexuality and Liberation.* Copyright © 1984 by The Pilgrim Press. Reprinted by permission of The Pilgrim Press.

"The Rising of the Loaf," by Susan F. Jarek-Glidden from *Wellsprings: A Journal for United Methodist Women.* Copyright © by Susan F. Jarek-Glidden. Reprinted with permission of the author.

"See Me How I Rise," by Marsie Silvestro from the recording *Circling Free.* Copyright © 1983 by Marsie Silvestro. Reprinted by permission of Marsie Silvestro.

"Even Crumbs Are Bread," from *Becoming Bread: Meditations on Loving and Transformation* by Gunilla Norris. Copyright © 1993 by Paulist Press, Inc., New York/Mahwah, New Jersey. Used with permission of Paulist Press, www.paulistpress.com.

Crossroads and Thresholds

Excerpt from *Sacred Spaces: Stations On a Celtic Way* by Margaret Silf. Copyright © 2001 by Margaret Silf. Published by Lion Hudson, Oxford, England. Reprinted by permission of Margaret Silf.

"Gather the Dreamers," by Kathy Sherman, CSJ, from her recording *Gather the Dreamers.* Reprinted with permission, courtesy of www.ministryofthearts.org.

Excerpt from *The Making of a Mind: Letters from a Soldier Priest* by Pierre Teilhard de Chardin, SJ. Copyright © 1961 by Editions Bernard Grasset, English translation copyright © 1965 by William Collins Sons & Co. Ltd. and Harper & Row Publishers, Inc., New York. Reprinted by permission of Georges Borchard, Inc.

Changing the Face of Aging

"Myself Growing Older," by Marsie Silvestro from the recording *In Avalon.* Copyright © 1995 by Marsie Silvestro. Reprinted by permission of the author.

Excerpt from *Women Who Run with the Wolves: Myths and Stories of the Wild Woman Archetype* by Clarissa Pinkola Estés. Copyright © 1992 by Clarissa Pinkola Estés. Reprinted by permission of Random House, Inc.

Excerpt from "How Could Anyone," by Libby Roderick from the recording *If You See a Dream.* Copyright © 1988 by Libby Roderick. Reprinted by permission of Turtle Island Records, Anchorage, Alaska, www.libbyroderick.com.

Streams of Wellness

Summer: Unburying Wonder

Fall: A Solemn Harvest

Winter: Sabbath

Poem by David Sluyter from the anthology *Prayers for a Thousand Years*. Reprinted by permission of David Sluyter.

"Just to Be," by Colleen Fulmer and the Loretto Spirituality Network. Copyright © by Colleen Fulmer. Reprinted by permission of Colleen Fulmer and the Loretto Spirituality Network.

Excerpt from "Holy Time, Holy Timing," by Jean M. Blomquist, from *Weavings,* January/February 1991. Copyright © 1991 by *Weavings* Magazine. Reprinted by permission of Jan M. Blomquist.

"The Avowal," by Denise Levertov, from *Oblique Prayers*. Copyright © 1984 by Denise Levertov. Reprinted by permission of New Directions Publishing Corp.

"Lullabye" by Cris Williamson. Copyright © 1992 by Cris Williamson, published by Bird Ankles Music, Wolf Moon Inc. Reprinted with permission of Cris Williamson.

Spring: Growing Pains

An excerpt from "Mud Season," from *Selected Poems of May Sarton* by May Sarton, edited by Serena Sue Hilsinger and Lois Brynes. Copyright © 1978 by May Sarton. Used by permission of W. W. Norton & Company, Inc.

"God Who Gardens," by Colleen Fulmer and the Loretto Spirituality Network from the recording *Her Wings Unfurled*. Copyright © 1989 by Colleen Fulmer. Reprinted by permission of Colleen Fulmer and the Loretto Spirituality Network.

Excerpt from *The Feminine Face of God: The Unfolding of the Sacred in Women* by Sherry Ruth Anderson and Patricia Hopkins. Copyright © 1991 by Sherry Ruth Anderson and Patricia Hopkins. Reprinted by permission of Bantam Books, a division of Random House, Inc.

Excerpt from *Dance of the Spirit* by Maria Harris. Copyright © 1989 by Maria Harris. Reprinted with permission of Bantam Books, a division of Random House, Inc.

"Rise Up, Child of the Earth," by Pat Kozak, CSJ, from *More Than Words: Prayers and Ritual for Inclusive Communities* by Pat Kozak and Janet Schaffram. Copyright © 1988 by Pat Kozak and Janet Schaffram. Reprinted by permission of Pat Kozak.

"See Me How I Rise," by Marsie Silvestro from *Circling Free*. Copyright © 1983 by Marsie Silvestro. Reprinted by permission of Marsie Silvestro.

ADDITIONAL BOOKS ON PRAYER AND SPIRITUALITY

And the Dance Goes On
An Anthology of Australian Catholic Women's Stories
by the Commission for Australian Catholic Women

A remarkable collection of stories from Down Under, told by contemporary Catholic women about their faith experience. 254-page paperback, $14.95

A Contemporary Celtic Prayer Book
by William John Fitzgerald
with a Foreword by Joyce Rupp

Done with a Celtic sensibility, using ancient and contemporary prayers, this unique prayer book contains a simplified Liturgy of the Hours plus Celtic blessings, prayers and rituals for special occasions. 148-page paperback, $9.95

Allegories of Heaven
An Artist Explores the "Greatest Story Ever Told"
by Dinah Roe Kendall
with "The Message" text by Eugene H. Peterson

Contemporary English artist Dinah Roe Kendall offers a vibrant visual retelling of the full scope of Jesus' ministry through her figurative and narrative paintings, accompanied by Eugene Peterson's widely acclaimed contemporary rendering of the Bible. 100-page, four-color hardcover, $14.95

Running into the Arms of God
Stories of Prayer/Prayer as Story
by Patrick Hannon

Stories of prayer in everyday life tied to the traditional hours of the monastic day: matins, lauds, prime, terce, sext, none, vespers, compline. 128-page hardcover, $15.95; paperback, $11.95

Prayers from Around the World and Across the Ages
compiled by Victor M. Parachin

A wealth of sublime, reverent and poignant prayers from many of the world's greatest spiritual practitioners, preceded by a one-paragraph biography of the person who composed it. 160-page paperback, $9.95

Available from booksellers or call 800-397-2282
www.actapublications.com